Children's Classics, Critically
by Philip Nel and Melanie Ramdarshan Bold, Series Editors

When adults re-read a children's book, we might seek comfort from imaginary worlds we visited during (what we remember as) a less complicated time. But we might also find ourselves pausing to re-read the words and pictures, intrigued by all that we missed when we were children. The *Children's Classics, Critically* series is for the readers who pause—those adults who enjoy revisiting a "classic" from their youth, and who are willing to complicate their relationship with that classic.

In our series title, *Critically* has a double valance: children's books are both vital ("mission critical") parts of our lives and merit thoughtful analysis. Since we encounter them when we are beginning to figure out who we are, books for young people can leave an outsized impression on our imaginations. Children's books have much to teach us about how power works, and why we might want to question what society teaches us to think of as normal or ordinary. *Children's Classics, Critically* encourages us to reexamine our assumptions about books for young readers. Some children's classics are problematic, some are not problematic, and most are somewhere in between. (The books in the series understand that, while art is political, art cannot be reduced to politics.)

In our series, "classic" denotes a children's or YA book (or series) that is widely read and/or critically acclaimed, *usually* published at least 20 years prior to the *Children's Classics, Critically* volume's publication date. We specify "*usually* at least 20 years prior" for two reasons. First, children's books can attain classic status within a generation. Once child readers become adults, they pass it on to the children in their lives—their own children, niblings, students, and others. Second, the "*usually*" enables this series to include more books by creators from underrepresented groups, since more such works have been published in recent years. To build diversity into the structure of this series, at least three of every ten *Children's Classics, Critically* volumes focus on a book by an artist or writer from a socially marginalized group. One of those three will leverage that *usually*. Also written or illustrated by a member of an underrepresented group, this book will be critically acclaimed and at least five years old. In these ways, our series will also help promote future classics that diversify what young people read.

Finally, *Children's Classics, Critically* recognizes that books for children and young adults have much to give those of us who are no longer their target audience. In addition to being works of art in their own right, books for young readers provide heuristics for thinking about the world. They deal with the fundamental things that we faced as children and contend with as adults. In children's books, there is art, wisdom, beauty, melancholy, hope, and insight for readers of *all* ages.

How to Draw the World

How to Draw the World

Harold and the Purple Crayon *and the Making of a Children's Classic*

PHILIP NEL

OXFORD
UNIVERSITY PRESS

OXFORD
UNIVERSITY PRESS

Oxford University Press is a department of the University of Oxford.
It furthers the University's objective of excellence in research, scholarship,
and education by publishing worldwide. Oxford is a registered trade mark of
Oxford University Press in the UK and in certain other countries.

Published in the United States of America by Oxford University Press
198 Madison Avenue, New York, NY 10016, United States of America.

Library of Congress Cataloging-in-Publication Data
Names: Nel, Philip, 1969– author.
Title: How to draw the world : Harold and the purple crayon
and the making of a children's classic / Philip Nel.
Description: New York : Oxford University Press, 2024. |
Series: Children's classics, critically | Includes bibliographical
references and index. | Summary: "How to Draw the World: Harold
and the Purple Crayon and the Making of a Children's Classic presents
the key concepts surrounding the children's book Harold and the
Purple Crayon written by Crockett Johnson. It explores several questions
regarding the nature of reality and creative expression during the
Cold War. Picture books are many people's introduction to looking
closely while also acting as a portable gallery that has a democratic art form.
How to Draw the World also highlights the success of Johnson's book,
particularly its design choices, Garamond typeface, and circulation around
the world. It also considers how Johnson overcame his editor's initially
lukewarm reaction"—Provided by publisher.
Identifiers: LCCN 2024019082 | ISBN 9780197777596 (hardback) |
ISBN 9780197777619 (epub)
Subjects: LCSH: Johnson, Crockett, 1906–1975. Harold and the purple crayon. |
Johnson, Crockett, 1906–1975—Criticism and interpretation. | Johnson,
Crockett, 1906–1975—Influence. | Art in literature. | Imagination in
literature. | Creative ability in children. | Picture books for
children—History.
Classification: LCC PS3519.O224 Z773 2024 | DDC 813/.52—dc23/eng/20240816
LC record available at https://lccn.loc.gov/2024019082

DOI: 10.1093/oso/9780197777596.001.0001

Sheridan Books, Inc., United States of America

Contents

Color Images

C1. Crockett Johnson's drawing of his proposed "Five-Inch Shelf," c. 1950s. Image courtesy of Northeast Children's Literature Collection, Dodd Center, University of Connecticut. Reproduced courtesy of The Ruth Krauss Foundation, Inc.

C2. Paul Klee, *Young Moe*, 1938. Colored paste on newspaper mounted on burlap, 20 7/8 x 27 5/8 in. The Phillips Collection, Washington, DC, Acquired 1948. © 2023 Artists Rights Society (ARS), New York.

C3. Crockett Johnson, brown color separation page (for "One evening, ..." two-page spread). Image courtesy of the Northeast Children's Literature Collection, University of Connecticut. Reproduced courtesy of The Ruth Krauss Foundation, Inc.

C4. Crockett Johnson, purple color separation page (for same two-page spread). Image courtesy of the Northeast Children's Literature Collection, University of Connecticut. Reproduced courtesy of The Ruth Krauss Foundation, Inc.

C5. Included with Helen M. Lothian's letter, a page from *Harold's Fairy Tale*, embellished by unknown artist. Image courtesy of Harper Collins.

C6. Crockett Johnson, *Squared Circle*, c. 1969. Photo by Dane Webster. Reproduced courtesy of Philip Nel.

C7. Megan Montague Cash, color simulations: from 100% purple to 5% purple, from 100% brown to 5% brown.

C8. Cover for Chinese translation. Translated by Liang Lin. Hsinex International Corporation, 1987.

C9. Cover: *Tullemand og det Violette Farvekridt*. Translated into Danish by Bibi and Thomas Winding. Copenhagen: Gyldendal, 2000.

C10. Cover: *Ich mach mir meine eigne Welt*. First German translation. Translator unknown. Walter-Verlag AG, c. 1970.

C11. Cover: *Harold und die Zauberkreide*. Translated by Anu Stohner. Carl Hanser Verlag, 2012.

Introduction

How to Read Harold

Crockett Johnson's *Harold and the Purple Crayon* (1955) was Prince's favorite childhood book. It is why Prince played purple guitars, favored purple fashion, and strongly identified with the color purple. *Harold* has inspired improvisational theatre, experiments in virtual reality, and Pulitzer-Prize-winning author Richard Powers to become a writer. Upon receiving the Caldecott Medal for *Jumanji* (1981), the classic picture book that would launch a film franchise, Chris Van Allsburg thanked "Jan Vermeer, for the way he used light; ... Federico Fellini, for making films that look the way they do; ... and Harold, for his purple crayon."

Harold and the Purple Crayon has sold more than five and a half million copies, been translated into fourteen languages, and launched six more Crockett Johnson books chronicling Harold's adventures (1956–1963), as well as a seventh (2020) not created by Johnson. It has inspired an animated cartoon (1959), an Emmy-winning TV series (2001–2002), a board game (2001), an iPad app (2011), two-stage adaptations (1990, 2009), a feature film (2024), and many artists. Harold is a cultural phenomenon and a window into the creative mind.

It's such an influential book because *Harold and the Purple Crayon* is one of the most succinct expressions of imaginative possibility ever created. Coming from Johnson's biographer (me), that claim may sound like hyperbole. But consider: the book shows how the mind can change the world, how dreams can make realities. It tells readers that, though they may be subject to forces

How to Draw the World: Harold and the Purple Crayon *and the Making of a Children's Classic.* Philip Nel, Oxford University Press. © Oxford University Press 2024. DOI: 10.1093/oso/9780197777596.003.0001

**Artist Crockett Johnson as
drawn by Harold.**

Figure 1. Crockett Johnson, self-portrait as Harold, 1950s. Image
courtesy of the Smithsonian Institution.

beyond their control, they can improvise, invent, draw a new
path. Yes, there are many earlier works that explore boundaries
between real and imagined worlds. In Chuck Jones's *Duck Amuck*
(1953), a mischievous animator (revealed at the end to be Bugs
Bunny) keeps scrambling Daffy Duck's reality. In René Magritte's
The Human Condition 1 (1933), an easel partially blocks the view
through a window *and* seems to render the "real" landscape it
obscures: however, since both easel and landscape emerge only
within the canvas of Magritte's larger painting, the work raises the
question of why and where we mark the borders of the "real."
Though not the first to pursue this idea, Johnson distills it into its
simplest and most profound form—using only a child artist, a
crayon, and a blank page. Explaining why *Harold and the Purple*

Crayon is the children's art book she recommends above all others, Jackson Pollock-biographer Deborah Solomon says that Harold tells us "one well-worn, stubby crayon could allow you to dream up a whole universe. Which of course it can. There's no better art history lesson than that."

As will become clear in the following pages, *Harold and the Purple Crayon* is a small book about big ideas. It raises questions about the nature of reality; creative expression during the Cold War; the implied audience of children's literature; abstract art versus representational art; and the color of crayons, ink, and people. All of these questions depend upon how children's picture books work—in this case, the apparent invisibility of Johnson's design choices, the limits imposed by the offset color lithography printing process, the history of the crayon, and the book's circulation into the hands of many real children around the world.

So, one goal of this book is to take the reader on an illustrated tour through what makes *Harold and the Purple Crayon* work, including its small size, Harold's clear line, Johnson's carefully planned improvisation, the Garamond typeface (yes, even the typeface!), the real "Harolds" who inspired the title character, how Johnson overcame his editor's initially lukewarm reaction, the role of the book's three colors (purple, brown, white), and whether or not the tan-hued Harold himself is a child of color. In the process, this book—the working title of which was "How to Read Harold"—also offers a primer on the art and design of children's picture books.

Children may have less height, vocabulary, and power than adults do. But children's books are not a lesser art form. As Nathalie op de Beeck writes, the picture book depends upon a "complex interdependency of visuals, words, and sequence." Though people new to the study of picture books often say that the pictures illustrate the words, they do no such thing. There can be no one-to-one correspondence between text and image because, first, that would make for a boring book, and second, words and images do not communicate in the same ways. What sort of chair does the word "chair" conjure in your mind? If I asked you to imagine a chair, would you see a wicker seat with a back made of two concentric loops, a solid plastic chair, a metal-and-canvas butterfly chair, or one of those plastic office chairs on wheels? Or perhaps you envision an Eames chair, a chaise lounge, a bean-bag chair, or the "high-backed chair" that Harold draws at the end of *Harold's Fairy Tale* (the second book in Johnson's series)? Or maybe something else entirely? In picture books, as William Moebius reminds us, "Pictures and words together are treated as semiautonomous and mutually attractive chains of meaning rather than as fixed images serving as supplement to meanings fixed in words." Building on the complex relationship between words and images, the picture book is both meticulously designed and (often) mass-produced. It is a flexible narrative art usually created by adults but enjoyed by readers of any age. As Barbara Bader puts it, the picture book is "text, illustration, total design; an item of manufacture and a commercial product; a social, cultural, and historical document."

This book unfolds as a series of microhistories that ripple outward from Johnson's book into art, design, politics, biography, children's literature, and beyond. The chapters are deliberately brief because, like Harold's art, they strive to explore many ideas with precision. There are many ideas because Crockett Johnson was a polymath and, as Harold's journey suggests, the creative process lacks clearly identifiable boundaries. Imagination's inherent unruliness and Johnson's ceaseless curiosity create many occasions when (like Harold) we will need to leave one path to draw a new one.

There are many such paths because the sustained attention that inspired this book has also expanded its scope. As Jenny Odell writes of the need for attentiveness more generally, "Context is what appears when you hold your attention open long enough; the longer you hold it, the more context appears." Johnson's book

COVER DRAWING FROM "HAROLD AND THE PURPLE CRAYON"
CROCKETT JOHNSON

Figure 2. Crockett Johnson, original cover drawing for *Harold and the Purple Crayon*, c. 1954. Image courtesy of the Smithsonian Institution. Reproduced courtesy of The Ruth Krauss Foundation, Inc.

has held my attention for most of my life. I first read *Harold and the Purple Crayon* fifty years ago, began writing about Crockett Johnson twenty-five years ago, and conceived of writing this—what I was then calling "a biography of a book"—ten years ago. The longer I've looked, the more contexts have appeared.

That said, looking closely does not require years. You need only focus and a willingness to ask questions. I hope my small book about a smaller one both models the pleasures of sustained attention and inspires you to look closely at art that interests you—picture books, of course, but really any kind of art. When you look, listen, or read closely, what questions does the art invite? Which questions from my book will work for you? What new questions will you need to ask?

As this book suggests, picture books are the ideal place to begin looking closely because in addition to being many people's introduction to visual art, a picture book is a portable art gallery. It is a more democratic art form, requiring only a library card, instead of, say, admission (and thus proximity) to a gallery. True, access to a library cannot be taken for granted: in the UK, Conservative and Lib Dem austerity measures led to the closure of 800 libraries between 2010 and 2020. In the US, budget cuts combined with rightwing attacks on diverse children's books are putting libraries in danger, too. However and at least for the present, libraries remain more accessible than galleries. In 2017, 49 percent of Americans visited a library, but only 24 percent went to a museum. As one of our earliest aesthetic experiences, picture books shape our perception of what art is and why it matters. As some of the first narratives we read (or have read to us), picture books show us how stories can make sense of the world and, in the case of *Harold and the Purple Crayon*, how we can create stories to guide us through that world. As Shaun Tan says of literature for children more generally, "Like a child daubing a paintbrush, it's just enough to know that even the most modest scribble or wordplay can at any moment lead to a simple but profound realization: the world is just what you make of it, a big, unfinished picture book inside your head."

This book takes *Harold and the Purple Crayon* as a case study of what we miss when we underestimate, trivialize, or simply fail to examine the art and design of the picture book. Indeed, *Harold*'s deceptively transparent aesthetic makes it ideal for such an inquiry because, at first glance, the book looks self-explanatory. What more can be said about a boy, a crayon, and the moon?

Here are thirty answers to that question.

1

A Child-Sized Book

Pick up the book and hold it in your hands. *Harold and the Purple Crayon* is 7.75 inches (19.66 cm) tall and 6.25 inches (15.88 cm) wide. But that's 38 percent larger than its original publication size. In 1998, HarperCollins re-launched the *Harold* books in what it called a "bold and bigger trim size along with bright and engaging treatments of the original cover art." For *Harold and the Purple Crayon*, "bright and engaging" meant coloring Harold's white jumper *blue*—a color darker than white. More importantly, though, the book's new dimensions mean that it no longer fits as easily into a small child's hands. When published in 1955, *Harold and the Purple Crayon* was 6 inches (15.25 cm) tall by 5 inches (12.7 cm) wide. Creating the book's dimensions, Crockett Johnson considered his audience: as Beatrix Potter did, he designed the book's proportions to match children's proportions. A smaller size for smaller hands.

In making the book small, Johnson also gestures to the long history of miniature books for children. In the sixteenth century, English publishers began producing Thumb Bibles—abridged and illustrated adaptations of the Bible intended for young readers. Later, famous artists and authors created small books, notably Kate Greenaway's *Alphabet* (c. 1885) and Paris publisher P. Pairault's ten-volume collection of fables and fairy tales (1895–1898), all of which could be housed in a miniature bookcase designed by the publisher. The idea of miniature libraries for children dates to at least 1800, when English publisher John Marshall created *The Infant's Library* (1800), which, as Veryeri Alaca writes, "encouraged children to read by means of sixteen

How to Draw the World: Harold and the Purple Crayon *and the Making of a Children's Classic.* Philip Nel, Oxford University Press. © Oxford University Press 2024. DOI: 10.1093/oso/9780197777596.003.0002

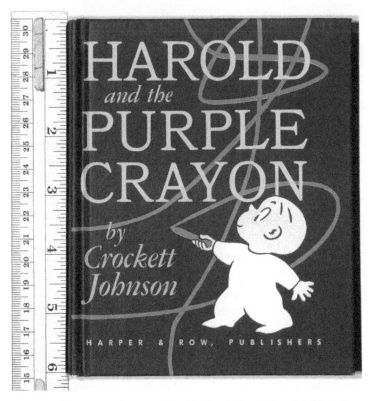

Figure 3. There is a photograph of the book *Harold and the Purple Crayon*. Image courtesy of Northeast Children's Literature Collection, Dodd Center, University of Connecticut. Reproduced courtesy of The Ruth Krauss Foundation, Inc.

illustrated volumes housed in a wooden bookcase in the shape of a toy house."

In the early 1950s, Johnson even drew up his own plans for miniature libraries. Calling it "The Five-Inch Shelf," he envisioned "a series of Tiny Golden Books…packed in plastic bookshelves five inches wide" (see C1). Each plastic shelf could stand on its own or interlock with other shelves in the series "to form a multi-shelf bookcase." He emphasized that the bookshelves should contain "worthwhile and entertaining books for younger children," and suggested they be organized around "classic" themes, such as selections from *Alice in Wonderland*, "Simple Science," "Lear Jingles," "Sleep Songs," "First Books of Industry (cow to bottle, sheep to coat, etc.)," and "Street Game Songs (farmer in the dell, etc.)." Designing the books for the not-yet-literate, he recommended different-colored spines "so that a particular volume may be found on the shelf by the non-reading child." Johnson even imagined an advertising campaign drawn by *New Yorker* cartoonists Whitney Darrow or Perry Barlow showing "the embarrassment of a baby in a carriage" who had "'not said a word' at the party (all because of his unfamiliarity with the 'Five-Inch Shelf')." Conceding that his promotion idea "may not be exactly right," he stressed the idea "behind it is a launching of the product in a 'smart' way." Though the product never did launch, the idea highlights both Johnson's creativity and his belief in good books for young people.

2

"Taking a line for a walk"

In the opening pages, Harold's scribbles are abstract art. They are not random. They have form. A sense of composition. They are more Paul Klee or Saul Steinberg than 3-year-old child. Like some of Klee's late work (C2), Harold's subject may be oblique, but his energetic line is precise. Like Steinberg, Harold is both playful and purposeful, creating an abstraction that has both the stability of architecture and the velocity of emotion. So, the book begins with paradox—the apparently random crayon strokes of a small boy that have the careful composition you'd expect from a great artist. The more I stare at the opening pages, the more I think that, in the lineage of bold line as fine art, Harold is the missing link between Keith Haring and Paul Klee, the latter of whom once described drawing as "taking a line for a walk." This is exactly what Harold does at the beginning of *Harold and the Purple Crayon*.

Many moments in Klee's *Pedagogical Sketchbook* (1925, published in English in 1953) resonate so strongly with *Harold and the Purple Crayon* that I want to claim Johnson knew Klee's little book. The first moments are the first two sentences: "An active line on a walk, moving freely, without goal. A walk for a walk's sake." Klee's example of a mountain as "freer movement and dynamic position" looks ahead to Harold's mountain-climbing in his first adventure and stair-climbing in his second, *Harold's Fairy Tale* (1956). Klee's "tightrope-walker is emphatically concerned about his balance"; tightrope-walking Harold's *lack* of sufficient concern about *his* balance launches the narrative of *Harold's Circus* (1959). Klee's example of how receding railroad tracks persuade the eye to "see" three dimensions strongly echoes the climatic visual illusion of

How to Draw the World: Harold and the Purple Crayon *and the Making of a Children's Classic.* Philip Nel, Oxford University Press. © Oxford University Press 2024. DOI: 10.1093/oso/9780197777596.003.0003

A Picture for Harold's Room (1960), in which Harold steps off the railway he has drawn, and suddenly realizes that his apparent smallness is all a trick of perspective.

But whether or not Johnson read *Pedagogical Sketchbook*, he and Klee had a shared understanding of how *line* works in art. Klee's lecture on his "Creative Credo" (1920, but not translated into English until 1961) reads like the prospectus for a Harold book. Inviting his readers on "a little journey into the land of fuller understanding," Klee proposes that "the first act of movement" be a "line." Then, "After a short while, we stop to get our breath," followed by a "glance back to see how far we have already gone (countermovement)." When "a river seeks to hinder us, we use a boat (wavy motion)"—just as Harold does when "over his head in an ocean." Echoing the conclusion of *Harold and the Purple Crayon*, Klee's sequence concludes when "we come to our original lodging. Before we fall asleep, a number of memories come back to us, for a short trip of this kind leaves us full of impressions."

3

Carefully Planned Improvisation

Harold's trip begins with his decision to take a line for a walk: "One evening, after thinking it over for some time, Harold decided to go for a walk in the moonlight." He draws a moon. He draws a path. Like his creator, Harold is a nocturnal, bald, artist. But Harold is also *not* like his creator. There's a tension between the narrator's level of diction and a typical 3-year-old's choice of words: "after thinking it over for some time" implies a perspective and degree of planning that we might not expect someone as young as Harold to have. Yet he does manage to draw one large picture in which no line is wasted, and nothing erased. His apparently spontaneous drawing must be the result of a great deal of "thinking it over." Or, rather, it's the result of Crockett Johnson creating a character whose improvisation is carefully planned. Another paradox: Though a meticulously designed book, *Harold and the Purple Crayon* presents itself as casual, unrehearsed, "easy." This was Johnson's aim and his bane: he was annoyed that people didn't notice how clever his work was, but the invisibility of his artifice is precisely what makes the book so powerful.

The production of the book underscores his meticulousness and the complexity of assembling this apparently simple book. To get it ready for production, Johnson had all the text set in type, and then drew sixty numbered Harolds, each one in a different position, and in a larger size than the book required. Placing all Harolds on a single sheet, he had a photostat made, reducing them to the size right for the book. Next, to create the paste-up, Johnson cut out the Harolds from the photostat and the text from the type-set pages. For each two-page spread, he made two sheets, all in

How to Draw the World: Harold and the Purple Crayon *and the Making of a Children's Classic.* Philip Nel, Oxford University Press. © Oxford University Press 2024. DOI: 10.1093/oso/9780197777596.003.0004

Figure 4. A page of Harolds from *Harold's ABC*. Johnson followed a similar process for *Harold and the Purple Crayon*, but I have not been able to find that page (or pages) of Harolds. Image courtesy of the Library of Congress. Reproduced courtesy of The Ruth Krauss Foundation, Inc.

black on white. On one (C3), he pasted a Harold (one per page) and the typeset text. On the other (C4), he drew the path of the purple crayon. On the one, he wrote "(BROWN)" to indicate that the outlines of Harold's body and the Garamond typeface will be brown. On that same one, he wrote "10% OF BROWN ON BLUE" to indicate that, via a filter that screens out 90 percent of the brown, a light brown (10 percent of full brown) would be printed on top of the blue watercolor wash he had applied to Harold's face and hands. On the other one, he has written "(PURPLE)" to indicate the black line for the crayon will in fact be in purple. When, in two separate stages (one for brown, one for purple), the printer applied each of these colors, the final page would show a tan-complexioned boy, outlined in brown, drawing with a purple crayon. Johnson's graphic precision creates Harold's spontaneity.

As Johnson once said, "Never overlook the art of the seemingly simple."

4

Type

So much aesthetic experience derives from those features of design that rarely reach a reader's conscious awareness—such as *Harold*'s Garamond typeface. It is likely the influence of Arthur Rushmore (1883–1955), a book designer, typographer, and head of Harper & Brothers' Book Production and Manufacturing from the late 1920s until his retirement in 1950. His favorite typeface was Garamond, and, though he no longer worked at Harper, his aesthetic influence lingered. Named for French typographer Claude Garamond (c. 1480–1561), the typeface emerged in the 1540s and, as journalist Simon Garfield says, "marked a final transition from gothic letters to the roman alphabet we recognize today." Aesthetically, Garamond is—to again borrow Garfield's words— "highly legible roman type," "respectable yet warm," "full of contrast and movement with a precision of line and elegant serifs."

While its warmth, movement, and precision befit a dreamy journey rendered in Johnson's precise line, Garamond's most powerful effect on *Harold and the Purple Crayon* is the invisibility of its legibility. Readers see the words and not the typeface. Its apparent transparency derives as much from the design as it does from the frequency of its use. A popular typeface for centuries, Garamond appears in many children's books, from H. A. Rey's *Curious George* (Harper, 1941) to the Dr. Seuss books (Vanguard, 1937–1938; Random House, 1939–1991) to the US editions of the *Harry Potter* series (Scholastic, 1998–2007).

In the 1940s, one popular measure of a typeface's legibility was the "blink test": eyes under strain blink more frequently. Readers who took the test were presented with the same text but in

How to Draw the World: Harold and the Purple Crayon *and the Making of a Children's Classic.* Philip Nel, Oxford University Press. © Oxford University Press 2024. DOI: 10.1093/oso/9780197777596.003.0005

different fonts, their involuntary blinks monitored carefully. The types that received the fewest blinks—the ones that fared best—were Garamond, Bembo, and Bodoni (the latter two, respectively, a descendant and cousin of Garamond). All three have been in frequent use for centuries. So, when we look at Garamond's familiar face and clean lines, its style seems to dissolve, leaving behind only pure words. This is an illusion, but an effective one for a tale that acknowledges illusion's role in creating (what we think of as) reality.

5

Blurring Boundaries

Art & Life

The next two pages introduce the book's central innovation—that the central character, standing on a blank page, will create his own universe. The horizontal line at left becomes the horizon line, as Harold extends it across to the right side of the page, adds a moon, and begins drawing a path. Johnson is not the first to make a character the creator of the work he inhabits. Earlier that same decade, Chuck Jones's *Duck Amuck* has Bugs Bunny drawing Daffy Duck, and Saul Steinberg's *New Yorker* drawings of the late 1940s and early 1950s include characters who draw themselves into (or out of) existence. Winsor McCay's *Little Nemo in Slumberland* of May 2, 1909, finds the title character gradually dreaming himself from a lush, three-dimensional reality into a two-dimensional child's sketch. The title page of Johnson's *A Picture for Harold's Room* references Magritte's *Human Condition 1*, another work that blurs the boundary between art and life.

The line between fantasy and reality is a central theme of Johnson's comic strip, *Barnaby* (1942–1952). Children see Mr. O'Malley—Barnaby's loquacious, endearing con-artist of a fairy godfather—and they see the other pixie characters. But most adults in the strip don't. They use their imaginations to explain away what they don't understand. Meanwhile, the children and readers know that the true cause of an event is O'Malley or one of his fellow pixies. For example, we know that the O'Malley behind O'Malley Enterprises is Barnaby's fairy godfather. The investors…do not. That said, for most of its run, the strip

How to Draw the World: Harold and the Purple Crayon *and the Making of a Children's Classic.* Philip Nel, Oxford University Press. © Oxford University Press 2024. DOI: 10.1093/oso/9780197777596.003.0006

Figure 5. Saul Steinberg, untitled *New Yorker* drawing, July 10, 1954.
© The Saul Steinberg Foundation/Artists Rights Society (ARS),
New York.

typically affirmed a clear boundary between real and imagined
events, visually verifying that the world of the pixies is real.
However, in the late 1940s, *Barnaby* often seems more interested
in blurring this boundary, developing that more capacious sense
of the imagination expressed in *Harold and the Purple Crayon*.
Inspired by Barnaby's interest in making clay models, his parents
take him to an art museum. Noting his interest, O'Malley takes
Barnaby back to the museum at night. Each artwork comes alive.
Myron's *Discobolus* throws his discus. Rodin's *The Thinker* takes a
break from thinking and starts reading a detective story.
Gainsborough's *Blue Boy* steps down from his canvas and swaps
hats with Barnaby. James McNeil Whistler's mother leaves her

A PURPLE CRAYON ADVENTURE

A Picture for Harold's Room

by CROCKETT JOHNSON

An I CAN READ Book®

HarperCollins*Publishers*

Figure 6. Title page from 1988 edition of *A Picture for Harold's Room* by Crockett Johnson. Illustrated by Crockett Johnson. Copyright © 1960 Crockett Johnson. Copyright renewed 1988 by Ruth Krauss Johnson. Used by permission of HarperCollins Publishers.

Figure 7. Crockett Johnson and Jack Morley, *Barnaby*, March 11, 1949. Image courtesy of Fantagraphics Books.

canvas to do some knitting. Meanwhile, a forlorn Abstraction laments, "NOBODY understands me." When these artworks come to life, they look ahead to Harold, who draws a purple landscape that becomes real—static but solid.

In November 1955, just two months after the publication of *Harold and the Purple Crayon*, Johnson sent his editor a review provided by his clipping service. Written by "Dave Marion Age 4," it reads, in full: "Harold can draw whatever he wants with his purple crayon, and then it really is." Johnson's accompanying note to his editor says, "Just in case you missed this—It's a very good review." He's joking, amused by the 4-year-old's brevity. But part of the joke is that this 15-word review gets at what's so startling about the book: Harold draws "with his purple crayon, and then it really is." I hear in this young reader's "and then it really is" some of the awe that may have drawn children to the book, and that continues to draw them to it today: its concise expression of how what we imagine can become real, its blurring of the boundary between art and life that pulls you into the story.

6

Windows, Part I

Motif & Metaphor

The window—the most frequently repeated image in *Harold and the Purple Crayon*—is a threshold not only between the safety of home and the adventure of leaving it, but between the real and the imaginary. In speculative fictions, windows often open into the fantastic. Peter Pan arrives through the Darling children's bedroom window, the ghost of Jacob Marley departs through Scrooge's bedroom window, and Mr. O'Malley enters through Barnaby's bedroom window. In populating the book with windows, Johnson evokes their long association with portals to the imagination. Suggesting an etymological link to this idea, architects Manfredo di Robilant and Niklas Maak note, "Old English sees the window as an escape hatch of the imagination, an eyethurl, eye hole."

While Johnson's creative choices may emerge instinctively, they are not accidental. It's not mere chance that Harold spends ten pages drawing windows—over three hundred of them in the "city full of windows" pages, plus at least sixteen on the "big building full of windows" and six on the house where he does not live. Nor is it luck that Harold's quest for home ends when he draws his bedroom window. Windows invite us to look through them and, in Johnson's book, to step through them and join Harold on his adventure.

How to Draw the World: Harold and the Purple Crayon *and the Making of a Children's Classic.* Philip Nel, Oxford University Press. © Oxford University Press 2024. DOI: 10.1093/oso/9780197777596.003.0007

7

"The scourge of crayon vandalism"

Harold also inspired some young readers to bring their own crayons into the story. In so doing, *Harold and the Purple Crayon* became what Robin Bernstein calls a "scriptive thing": It invites its readers to act. Specifically, it extends an invitation to join Harold in decorating the book's mostly white pages. In March 1958, Helen M. Lothian, Children's Librarian of Ontario's Niagara Falls Public Library, even sent Crockett Johnson some "evidence" of the "havoc" his book had caused: the final two pages from *Harold's Fairy Tale*, both generously embellished by a reader's crayon (C5). "We have been accused of becoming a passive audience," she wrote, "it must give you pleasure to have written books which inspire action." Though Lothian's tone makes me wonder if her letter was tongue-in-cheek, Johnson didn't read it that way. He had often heard versions of this complaint. Annoyed, Johnson drafted a long, satirical reply, claiming that his *Harold* books are in fact designed "to combat the scourge of crayon vandalism":

> A "Harold" book invites an average vandal to indulge himself vicariously, to sublimate his urge. Often the effect is so long-lasting that the next two or three books that fall into his hands are spared. When any such lapse occurs the organization no longer can depend on a member and he, finding himself with few assignments, usually begins to lose interest and he drops out. The object of course is to decimate the enemy's ranks, ultimately to make the dread organization of crayon vandals a thing of the past.

How to Draw the World: Harold and the Purple Crayon *and the Making of a Children's Classic.* Philip Nel, Oxford University Press. © Oxford University Press 2024. DOI: 10.1093/oso/9780197777596.003.0008

Niagara Falls Public Library

Niagara Falls, Ontario

March 13, 1958.

Mr. Crockett Johnson,
c/o Harper & Brothers,
49 East 33rd Street,
New York 16, N.Y., U.S.A.

Dear Mr. Johnson,

No doubt you are aware of the havoc you have
caused but I thought you might like to have
this evidence as a souvenir.

We have had other complaints: one child
refuses to us any crayon except the purple ones
and this means that there are hundreds of other
colours not used up.

We have been accused of becoming a passive
audience, it must give you pleasure to have
written books which inspire action.

Yours sincerely,

Helen M. Lothian

(Miss) Helen M. Lothian.

Figure 8. Letter from Helen M. Lothian to Crockett Johnson, March 13, 1958. Image courtesy of HarperCollins. Reprinted courtesy of the Niagara Falls (Ontario) Public Library.

Having gotten that off his chest, he sent the letter *not* to the librarian, but to his editor, asking if she thought his "long and labored comical joke" was or could become humorous enough "to serve any publicity purpose" by raising "a semi-humorous controversy about the series?" She did not.

April 13, 1958

Helen M. Lothian
Niagra Falls Public Library
Niagra Falls, Ontario

Dear Miss Lothian,

threatening

As the only author sufficiently aware of the nature of the menace ~~threatening~~ the destruction of our libraries to have thrown himself and his talents boldly into the struggle against it, I am staggered to learn that my efforts to combat the scourge of crayon vandalism not only can go unappreciated but actually can be misconstrued as the "cause" of the havoc I am so importantly engaged in stamping out. You have been taken in by the enemy.

Your letter reveals that you have no grasp of the problem that faces us and that you know very little about our opponents. Their organization, on the surface, is so apparently loose-knit and casual that I daresay you have not recognized it as an organization at all. Its members are disarmingly young, which tends to lead a superficial observer to laugh at the assertion that it has systematically been destroying the world's literature for centuries. But what do you think really happened to Ptolemy's library in Alexandria, and why, do you suppose, Gutenberg Bibles are so rare? To fully grasp how effectively the crayon vandals operate, consider how their organization maintains itself despite its necessarily enormous turnover in personnel. The average crayon vandal is eligible only for his most destructive period, not over two or three years. And yet, decade after decade, crayon vandalism has continued to grow. For a time fantastically increased book production seemed to keep pace. But a few years ago it became clear to me that, unless a means could be found to reduce the rate of the vandals' toll, we soon would reach a point at which destruction overtook production. A thorough study of crayon vandalism and crayon vandals was urgently indicated.

The average crayon vandal seems childlike and innocent, and actually he is. But there are millions like him, each with his small urge for destruction developed and channeled by the efficient hard core of the organization, by its precocious and dedicated leaders. These leaders are comparatively few in number and, without their vast horde of naive followers, of course could not carry on the work in anything except a very negligible manner. It was from this observation that I devised my strategy and went on to invent the tactical weapons for putting it into effect, the "Harold" books.

I gather you think the specimen of crayon vandalism you enclose is typical. I assure you, to the trained eye it is not. Significantly, the page is from "Harold's Fairy Tale" and, at a glance, the mutilations are the work of an old hand at the game, very likely a leader of considerable importance in the organization. The marks are both vindictive and a calculated attempt to confuse, to weaken our side's faith in the book. For such leaders immediately recognize a "Harold" book as the threat it is to them, a volume designed to deter their less perceptive colleagues and bring about disaffection in the ranks. That is precisely what the books do.

A book already marked up with crayon when it comes from the publisher not only tends to move an average crayon vandal with a jot of sporting blood in him to put

Figures 9 and 10.   Crockett Johnson's response to Lothian, April 13, 1958. Image courtesy of HarperCollins. Reprinted courtesy of The Ruth Krauss Foundation, Inc.

I want to claim that Lothian's letter represents a trend. Johnson suggests that it does when he tells his editor, "I have heard the gripe about the 'Harold' books before." Two otherwise favorable reviews of *Harold's Fairy Tale* also express concern that, as Joyce Elliot writes in *The Library Journal*, "Young children might be tempted to follow Harold's example and write on walls." Margaret

up his weapon and admit temporary defeat, but it also has a longer lasting
immobilizing effect. A "Harold" book invites an average vandal to indulge himself
vicariously, to sublimate his urge. Often the effect is so long-lasting that
the next two or three books that fall into his hands are spared. When any such
lapse occurs the organization no longer can depend on a member and he, finding
himself with few assignments, usually begins to lose interest and often he drops
out. The object of course is to decimate the enemy's ranks, ultimately to make
the dread organization of crayon vandals a thing of the past.

But it is much too soon to talk of total victory. British libraries only
last year recognized the books as a defense against their crayon vandals. This
year Holland's libraries installed a Dutch edition and other translations are
being rushed to press to protect the libraries of Switzerland, West Germany,
Denmark, and Sweden. This is merely a beginning. The road is fraught with
difficulty and prejudice. You, after reading this far and reconsidering your
impetuous letter, will be the first to agree that our opponents have not been
idle in beclouding the issue. It will be a matter of years, probably, before
world statistics on crayon marks per page, for the first time in history, show a
noticeable downward trend. But the day will come!

Forgive the exclamation point. I tend to become carried away. But I am sure
you will understand. And I hope, from now on, to have your continued understanding
and that of the Niagra Falls Public Library's entire staff.

*Sincerely,

Crockett Johnson

*Our slogan, which means, of course, without wax, the principle ingredient of our
opponents' weapons.

Figures 9 and 10. *Continued*

Sherwood Libby's *New York Herald Tribune* review even proposes that Harold himself issue a warning to young readers:
"When a hero like Harold...slashes away with a purple crayon,
perhaps he should warn admirers of his own size to ask for paper
before they go on a similar imaginative journey." Since I am the
sort of person who buys used copies of the *Harold* books, I can
confirm—anecdotally, at least—that some children accepted the
invitation to reach for their own crayons, and did draw in the
books' pages.

While I do not know whether the *Harold* books have incurred
more crayon vandalism than other children's books, I can see how
young readers might find all that blank space enticing. Harold
draws with a crayon on white paper. Many children have access to

crayons; the books' ample negative space must seem a welcome canvas on which to emulate Harold. As Peter Turchi observes, "Omissions, intended or unintended, provoke the imagination." The unmarked spaces on the books' pages have surely launched many creative journeys.

8

"I stubbed my toe on Harold and his damned purple crayon"

However, the *Harold* series almost did not launch at all. When the dummy for *Harold and the Purple Crayon* arrived on her desk in November 1954, Ursula Nordstrom—his editor and the Director of Harper & Brothers' Department of Books for Boys and Girls from 1940 to 1973—was puzzled. A decade ago, Johnson had illustrated his wife Ruth Krauss's popular *The Carrot Seed* (1945), but what was this *Harold and the Purple Crayon*? "I don't know what

11/22/54

Dear Dave:

The dummy of HAROLD AND THE PURPLE CRAYON came this morning, and I've just read it. I don't know what to say about it. It doesn't seem to be a good children's book to me but I'm often wrong - and this post-Children's Book Week Monday finds me dead in the head. I'd probably pass up TOM SAWYER today. Let me keep the dummy a few days, will you? I want Ann Powers to read it. She's young and fresh (not sassy, you understand) and less tired than I am. And I'd like to read it again myself when I'm a little more caught up.

I found myself asking such dumb questions - like where did he draw the moon and the path and the tree? And then when I got far enough to realize he was dreaming, OF COURSE, I was puzzled by the moon in the last picture. You can see from this heavy-handed comment that I didn't read the story with much imagination.

I hate to send you this sort of a nothing letter. But I wanted to send you some sort of word and this is the best I can do today. We'll keep the dummy a little longer and I'll write you again soon, or call you up.

Yours,

Ursula

Figure 11. Letter from Ursula Nordstrom to Crockett Johnson, November 22, 1954. Image courtesy of HarperCollins.

How to Draw the World: Harold and the Purple Crayon *and the Making of a Children's Classic.* Philip Nel, Oxford University Press. © Oxford University Press 2024. DOI: 10.1093/oso/9780197777596.003.0009

12/15/54

To Crockett Johnson
~~San~~ ~~Larkr~~ ~~St.,~~ ~~Rowayton~~

Dear Dave:

The typed up slightly revised
copy of HAROLD AND THE PURPLE CRAYON has just
come. Many many thanks. I think it is FINE,
and the little changes you made are just perfect.
Thanks for the part about the forest, and for all
the other little touches.

I'm awfully sorry my first reaction
to HAROLD was so ~~xx~~ luke warm and unchthusiastic.
As I wrote you, I was tired in my head. I really
think it is going to make a darling book, and I
certainly was wrong at first. This is a funny job.
The Harper children's books have had such a good
fall, so many on so many lists, etc. etc., and I
was feeling a little good - not satisfied, you
understand, but I thought gosh I'm really catching
on to things, I bet, and pretty soon it ought to
get easier. And then I stubbed my toe onHarold
and his damned purple crayon....

The contract is being drawn up -
and I'm sorry the typing is taking so long.

Yours,

Ursula

Figure 12. Letter from Ursula Nordstrom to Crockett Johnson,
December 15, 1954. Image courtesy of HarperCollins.

to say about it," Nordstrom wrote. "It doesn't seem to be a good
children's book to me but I'm often wrong—and this post-
Children's Book Week Monday finds me dead in the head. I'd
probably pass up *Tom Sawyer* today. Let me keep the dummy a
few days, will you?" She then gave the dummy to Harper reader
Ann Powers, who was also not immediately taken with it: "I don't
think it is anything sensational, but it is a little different."

Of course, both Powers and Nordstrom came around. You can even see Powers changing her mind *while* she is writing her reader's report. In her final paragraph she admits, "The more I look at the book, the more I like it," and she concludes, "This is undoubtedly one of those books which are indescribable in copy." Nordstrom apologized: "I think it is going to make a darling book, and I certainly was wrong at first." The Harper children's books, she said, were having "such a good fall" that she thought "gosh I'm really catching on to things, I bet, and pretty soon it ought to get easier. And then I stubbed my toe on Harold and his damned purple crayon...."

9

Children's Art

Nordstrom's initial ambivalence toward a story "drawn" by a child recalls debates over whether and when we value children's creativity. "Drawing like a child" can be both insult and praise. How many times have you heard someone dismiss modern art with the claim that "a 3-year-old child could have made that"? As Jonathan Fineberg points out, "The idea that modern art looks like something a child could do is one of the oldest clichés around." A German critic in 1933 dismissed the work of Paul Klee as "mad, infantile smearings." Contemporary critics of COBRA—an art movement (1948–1951) that drew inspiration from Klee, Joan Miró, and children's drawings—called their work "messy" and "childish," asserting that they had seen such work "before, made by children but then much better and much more spontaneously and unconsciously drawn."

That spontaneous, untutored style is precisely what drew Klee, Miró, Pablo Picasso, Wassily Kandinsky, Gabrielle Münter, and others in the modernist avant-garde both to collect and to emulate children's art. For them, "drawing like a child" was an aesthetic goal, not cause for censure. As Kandinsky wrote, "The child is still stranger to practical purposes, as it looks at everything with unfamiliar eyes and still has the undimmed ability to perceive things as such." In their own artworks, he and Münter incorporated figures from the children's drawings they collected. Other artists avoided direct imitation, instead developing a style that evokes children's artwork. In Klee's *Young Moe* (1938), over colored paste and newspaper, thick black lines gesture to the face of the Swiss composer, Albert Moeschinger, and suggest the energy of melody

How to Draw the World: Harold and the Purple Crayon *and the Making of a Children's Classic.* Philip Nel, Oxford University Press. © Oxford University Press 2024. DOI: 10.1093/oso/9780197777596.003.0010

(C2). Miro's lithograph *Young Girl* (1948) and poster for the International Exhibition of Surrealism (1947) each use simple geometric shapes as oddly proportioned abstractions of human bodies—as is characteristic of children's drawings.

A former (amateur) child artist himself, Johnson supports children's creativity, but does not romanticize children's art as more "real" or "pure" or "primitive." In *Harold and the Purple Crayon*, he most clearly gestures to a child's style of drawing when Harold draws living figures, such as the dragon, moose, porcupine, and policeman. In contrast, the diagonal lines of the path, the straight line of the mast, and the circle of the balloon have a precision uncharacteristic of young children's art. They are closest to Johnson's characteristic clear-line style—which Johnson himself described as "simplified, almost diagrammatic, for clear storytelling, avoiding all arbitrary decoration." As the sole figure in the book *not* created by the crayon, Harold embodies Johnson's style—and marks the sometimes subtle differences between the aesthetics of author and character. Ranging from the jagged-fingered, star-smocked cop to the smooth ellipse of the hot air balloon, Harold's style moves between "amateur child" and "professional adult," but never quite settles into either. As Edward Lear did in his books for children, Johnson takes inspiration from children's art without idealizing a child muse.

As Victoria Ford Smith notes, the childlike features of the art that Lear created for his nonsense books (starting with his *Book of Nonsense* in 1846) stand in sharp contrast to his very detailed paintings of landscapes and birds. An accomplished painter, Lear was known for his "extraordinary accuracy," winning "acclaim for his studies of birds, which he drew almost entirely from nature (paying careful attention to all details of feather and color)." However, in his books for children, the "chaotic energy" of his "childlike drawings feature uneven perspectives, imprecise forms, and lopsided figures balanced in impossible poses." The distinction between Johnson's style and Harold's style is more subtle than the difference between Lear's paintings and his children's books. However, in presenting a childish style as a valid aesthetic choice, both artists affirm children's creativity as valuable. In Lear's day, that sentiment was novel. In Johnson's day, the creative child was coming into vogue.

10

Postwar America Embraces Children's Creativity

Harold and the Purple Crayon and its sequels emerged when creative education was posited as a moral good—when the inherently creative romantic child could be nurtured, studied, quantified, and commodified. In the 1950s, US government agencies and private companies heralded "creativity as an untapped natural resource," as Amy F. Ogata has shown. Victor D'Amico, Director of Education at the Museum of Modern Art, created art classes in which he encouraged children *not* to copy other works (the common practice at the time), but to explore "their own imaginations in works of art." Elementary schools across the US promoted art education as fostering humanistic values, a democratic spirit, self-confidence, and the creativity necessary to success in life. Capitalizing on the surging interest in art education, Binney & Smith—makers of Crayola—found a huge market for their crayons. The company conducted free workshops for teachers, who in turn taught their students art projects that required (and thus encouraged the purchase of) Binney & Smith's crayons and finger paints. By the 1970s, the company "claimed some 70 percent of the American crayon market." Unsurprisingly, then, Johnson's crayon-wielding protagonist met a receptive audience.

One of the television shows to capitalize on the investment in children's creativity may have influenced Johnson, and should have been familiar to his Harper editors, too. The popular children's program *Winky-Dink and You* (1953–1957) not only encouraged young imaginations but was fully interactive. At the

How to Draw the World: Harold and the Purple Crayon *and the Making of a Children's Classic.* Philip Nel, Oxford University Press. © Oxford University Press 2024. DOI: 10.1093/oso/9780197777596.003.0011

Figure 13. *Winky-Dink and You.* Photo by CBS via Getty Images.

start of each episode, host Jack Barry told children to get their Winky-Dink kits (which had to be purchased), take out the "magic screen" (a piece of transparent vinyl), rub it with the erasing cloth, and affix it to the TV screen. Rubbing it with the cloth created static electricity which kept the plastic in place. Barry then asked children to use their "magic crayons" to draw on the screen, helping complete a picture. They might draw a bridge so that Winky-Dink could cross a river, or a ladder so that Winky-Dink could climb out of a hole. As in Johnson's *Harold and the Purple Crayon*, a child's crayon creates reality, and the boundary between imagined and real worlds is thin. Not only did children (the "you" in the show's title) interact with a TV program, but Barry, the

Figure 14. Crockett Johnson in the living room at his Rowayton, Connecticut, home. 1959. Image courtesy of the Smithsonian Institution. Reproduced courtesy of the *New Haven Register*.

show's human host, interacted with the animated Winky-Dink character—voiced by Mae Questel, the voice of Betty Boop and Olive Oyl in the 1930s. I doubt that Johnson was a regular viewer of this program: it aired on Saturday mornings at 10:30 am, and he tended to rise closer to noon. But *Winky-Dink and You* was also too popular for him to ignore, he had an interest in animation, and he did own a TV. In 1947, he became the first resident of Rowayton—the small Connecticut town where he lived—to buy a television set.

11

One, Two, Three Dimensions; or, "And the moon went with him"

Despite its broad narrative parallels with *Harold and the Purple Crayon*, *Winky-Dink* is less sophisticated than Johnson's book. Children's scribbly drawings on a TV screen clearly separate artist from medium. These children are just playing at altering reality. However, thanks to the stylistic consistency of Johnson's clear line, Harold and his artwork all inhabit the same reality. Their shared aesthetic allows Johnson to convince us that, for example, oscillating between two and three dimensions is perfectly normal. Or, at least, this oscillation—which begins at the moment when Harold draws the path—convinces most people. It initially puzzled Johnson's editor. Looking at Johnson's dummy, Nordstrom said, "I found myself asking such dumb questions—like <u>where</u> did he draw the moon and the path and the tree?" First among a list of "The parts I am not too sure of," Harper reader Ann Powers also named "the pathway at the beginning (too strange?)." It may be strange, but when Harold is standing in an empty void, it makes sense for him to draw a "long straight path." It's practical. It anchors him. It also creates the illusion of three dimensions in what has—up to this point—been two-dimensional space. Unlike most pre-schoolers, Harold understands the vanishing point.

In one sense, the observation that "he didn't seem to be getting anywhere on the long straight path" echoes such advice as "taking the road less traveled" or "getting off the beaten path." Harold's decision to leave it announces his creativity. In another sense, the observation is literally true. His drawing only appears to have three dimensions. He's actually on a flat page. The most he can do on this "path" is walk in place. To get anywhere, he needs to acknowledge the flatness of the page and walk off the path, into a new space, blank, and ready for his crayon.

As he departs from the path, "the moon went with him" suggests a three-dimensional reality—even though only *some* of Harold's drawings have three dimensions. The pies and picnic blanket are 3-D. The dragon and boat are 2-D. The balloon begins as one-dimensional (a curved line), becomes two-dimensional (a circle), and ends as three-dimensional (two ropes extending behind and two ropes in front). But its basket stays two-dimensional, as does the house it lands in front of. Yet these differing numbers of dimensions (often on the same page) don't seem inconsistent or out-of-place because the moon helps trick us into seeing these scenes in three-dimensional space. When we walk at night in the real, physical world, the moon seems to follow us. The moon is the only part of Harold's drawing that's able to move, hovering over his head, far off in the distance, as he walks along.

Though neither named in the title nor represented on the cover, the moon is as important as Harold and his crayon. Perhaps acknowledging the moon's key role in this trio, two later Harold books do feature the moon on the cover: next to a tightrope-walking Harold on *Harold's Circus* (1959) and as the final letter in his name on *Harold's ABC* (1963). The moon is Harold's companion throughout *Harold and the Purple Crayon*, and the third constant visual motif. After its introduction, the moon appears in every scene—along with the two other constants (Harold and his crayon). Harold might be read as a stand-in for the reader, the crayon as his (or our) imagination, and the moon a guiding light. Or, better: Harold is the artist, the crayon his medium, and the moon his muse.

12

The Moon

As the sole celestial body visible without a telescope even in the light-polluted skies of a city, the moon has long fascinated poets, artists, scientists, and children. A natural calendar, its waxing and waning marks the passage of time. That its cycle restarts every 27.3 days, just slightly less frequently than once a month, may be the reason it is called the moon. As Maggie Aderin-Pocock notes, *moon* seems a descendent of "an Old English word derived from the Germanic word *menon*, which in turn is thought to come from an Indo-European word, *menses*, meaning 'month' or 'moon.'" One of the earliest artistic representations of the moon, the Nebra Sky Disk—a two-dimensional metal-and-gold sculpture that dates to 1600 BCE—appears to be a lunar calendar used by Bronze Age astronomers. Some 3,200 years later, Galileo Galilei looked through his new telescope and created the first detailed sketches of the moon's surface, publishing them in his *Sidereus Nuncius* ("Starry Messenger," 1610) along with theories, descriptions, and drawings of other constellations.

Harold draws the moon in all seven *Harold* books. On the cover of *Harold's ABC*, he draws the "D" in "HAROLD" as a moon, the sole *Harold* book in which the moon is waxing. In making that claim, I'm assuming that Harold—like his author—is in Connecticut. In the northern hemisphere, the bright part of a waning moon's circumference is to the left, and the bright part of a waxing moon's circumference is to the right—like the "D" in "HAROLD." If you are reading this book or the *Harold* books in the southern hemisphere, then please reverse all "rights" and "lefts" in this paragraph. In using the directions "left" and "right,"

How to Draw the World: Harold and the Purple Crayon *and the Making of a Children's Classic.* Philip Nel, Oxford University Press. © Oxford University Press 2024. DOI: 10.1093/oso/9780197777596.003.0013

I am also assuming an evening moon when it is lit by sunlight from the west. The moon's brightness is a reflection of the sun's light and so its brightest side always faces in the direction of the sun.

Though the moon's phases are constantly changing, a full moon suggests completion, the end point of a cycle. In addition to distinguishing the moon from the consistently[1] spherical sun, drawing Harold's moon as waning or waxing reminds readers that it is always in process, in motion, on the move—just as Harold is. Its phases dependable and its glow reassuring, the moon is an ideal nighttime companion.

Perhaps the moon's regular fluctuations in visibility, the fact that it is both constant and changing, are part of what attracts and inspires humans—from Van Gogh's *Starry Night* (1889, which also features a crescent moon) to many works for children. "Hey diddle diddle, / The Cat and the Fiddle, / The Cow jump'd over the Moon," first published in eighteenth-century London, gains in Randolph Caldecott's nineteenth-century illustrations a vivid anthropomorphic crescent moon: At the edge of the horizon, it smiles as the cow completes its jump. In the most frequently republished of Winsor McCay's *Little Nemo in Slumberland* comics (from July 26, 1908), the legs of Nemo's bed grow and then walk out into the night, carrying Nemo and Flip along for the ride, a full moon illuminating eight of the sixteen panels. In Virginia Lee Burton's *The Little House* (1942), the moon both marks time and favors the rural: it is less visible amid city lights and returns as a welcome sign of the house's relocation to the country in the book's final pages.

Most famously of all, Margaret Wise Brown and Clement Hurd's *Goodnight Moon* (1947) features a full moon, visible through the window of the bunny-child's well-appointed bedroom. When Johnson was writing *Harold*, the book had not yet attained its spectacular popularity. He and Brown did have the same editor (Ursula Nordstrom) and Ruth Krauss knew and respected Brown's work; so, it's possible that he had seen

Goodnight Moon. On the other hand, a moon framed by a window is not unusual: the denouement of *Harold and the Purple Crayon* may remind readers of Hurd's illustration, but we don't know whether it's influence or coincidence.

I would like to say that Johnson's lunar fascination dates to his childhood, when he gazed at the moon from his bedroom window on the second floor of the two-story wood-frame house (where he and his family lived by the time he turned 6) in Corona, Queens. But that would be pure invention. My knowledge of his childhood is limited because, first, Johnson lacked any autobiographical impulse and threw most things away, and second, the lives of the poor leave behind fewer traces than the lives of the wealthy. He grew up working class, the son of immigrants—a Scots father and a German mother. To reconstruct his early life, I had only public records (census data, insurance company maps, city directories, telephone books), his own occasional remarks to interviewers, the history of Queens, his high school literary magazine, and my sole witness to his childhood—his sister Else Frank, who I interviewed two years before her death. All of that research was moonless.

Figure 15. Beneath a crescent moon, Barnaby meets Gus the (rather timid) Ghost: two panels from Crockett Johnson's *Barnaby* of January 30, 1943. Image courtesy of Fantagraphics Books.

But I can at least tell you that the moon first appears in Johnson's work in the final panel of the *Barnaby* comic from Thursday, June 11, 1942: a waning crescent lights the sky above Mr. O'Malley, in flight and unable to shake the angry parrot clinging to his jacket. A crescent moon often appears in the strip's night sky, either lighting the way for characters' adventures or framed by Barnaby's window.

The moon doesn't become a narrative interest for Crockett Johnson until he begins thinking about the possibility of space travel, first in *Barnaby* and then in the *Harold* books. In September 1951, Mr. O'Malley decides to build a rocket ship to fly himself to the moon, making space exploration the strip's central theme for the rest of that year. Six years later (the year of Sputnik), *Harold's Trip to the Sky* finds Harold on a rocket to the moon but shooting past it and landing on Mars. In *Harold's ABC*, Harold spends part of the alphabet on the moon: anticipating William Anders's famous "Earthrise" photo (taken from Apollo 8 in December 1968), Harold sees the earth from the perspective of the moon. To find his way back to Earth, he decides he "would have to ask the man in the moon, or the king, or whoever was in charge."

Like Harold, Crockett Johnson spent more waking hours with the moon than most people do. He was nocturnal, often drawing his comic strips or children's books as moonlight streamed through his window. During his decade of drawing *Barnaby*, he typically worked from 11 pm until 5 am the next morning: he would spend two nights writing the scripts for a week of strips, followed by two nights drawing them. When running late, Johnson would first thing in the morning bring the week's strips to his neighbor who, on his way to work in New York City, dropped them off at the syndicate. Also, like Harold, Johnson knew how to improvise under pressure. Metaphorically speaking, he too "always kept his wits and his purple crayon."

13

The Purple Crayon

In *Harold and the Purple Crayon*, there are three central items (boy, crayon, moon), and four central colors: Harold's 10 percent brown skin, the 100 percent brown outline and typeface, the white page and jumper, and the purple crayon. Why these colors? Why a *purple* crayon? The reticent Johnson only answered this question once: "Purple is the color of adventure." It's impossible to tell whether he was kidding, serious, or a bit of both. The word "purple" is more fun to say than green, blue, or orange. In nature, it's the color of some distant mountains, drawn by Harold in three of his seven books and famously inspiring the line "purple mountain majesties" in Katharine Lee Bates's lyric for "America, the Beautiful" (1910), an unofficial US national anthem.

Though a popular color today, purple was not widely available until the nineteenth century. Its high cost kept purple from all but the wealthy and powerful. Kassia St. Clair traces purple's close association with royalty—drawn by Harold in both *Harold's Fairy Tale* and *Harold's ABC*—to the birth of Caesarion ("Little Caesar"), the son of Cleopatra and Julius Caesar. To mark the occasion, Caesar "introduced a new toga, which only he was allowed to wear." The toga was dyed in Cleopatra's favorite color: Tyrian purple. In Caesar's day, one had to blend the liquid harvested from the glands of two varieties of Mediterranean shellfish: since each one contained a single drop, an ounce of dye required about 250,000 of these shellfish. Later variants of purple were equally arduous. Making archil, a dark-red purple dye brought (from the Levant) to Europe in the fourteenth century, required pounds of lichen "ground to a fine powder." As St. Clair says, "First

How to Draw the World: Harold and the Purple Crayon *and the Making of a Children's Classic.* Philip Nel,
Oxford University Press. © Oxford University Press 2024. DOI: 10.1093/oso/9780197777596.003.0014

a source had to be discovered, and because lichen populations proved so fragile, each site was quickly exhausted." It was not until the mid-nineteenth century that scientists at last discovered easier ways to synthesize shades of purple. Two of those shades—mauve and heliotrope—went in and out of English fashion in the latter half of that century. In the 1870s, French impressionists Degas, Monet, Cézanne, Pissarro, and others embraced a third shade, violet, using it in their paintings. By the end of the nineteenth century, purple had moved from royalty to the avant-garde, and from rarity to a necessary part of the artist's palette. You could even find it in a box of crayons.

Those, too, were difficult to mass produce until the nineteenth century. The word *crayon* blends the French *craie* (chalk) with the Latin word *creta* (earth) because, until the nineteenth-century invention of wax-based crayons, *crayon* referred to what we would today call *chalk*. Though creating art via combinations of pigment and wax dates to ancient Greece and Egypt, the technique was too labor-intensive for everyday use. It would take people like French lithographer Joseph Lemercier (in Paris, c. 1828) and Wrocław native Louis Prang (in the US, in the 1880s)—each of whom sold antecedents of modern wax crayons—to develop the technology, and then several American companies to bring the results to a broader public. By the mid-1910s, there were over a dozen US crayon manufacturers, but the top eight were: the American Crayon Company, Binney & Smith (makers of Crayola), the Franklin Crayon Company, Joseph Dixon Crucible (later Dixon-Ticonderoga), Milton Bradley (later famous for board games), the Munsell Color Company, the Prang Educational Company, and the Standard Crayon Company. For the most part, they were making these crayons for children, one of whom was very likely a young Crockett Johnson—who was born in 1906, and who (according to his sister) loved to draw so much that, when bored at church, would draw pictures in the margins of the hymnals.

There are three reasons that crayons quickly become associated with American childhood: the Prang Educational Company's interest in promoting art education, the Crayola company's development of non-toxic crayons, and the fact that commercially available wax crayons emerge just when the kindergarten movement reached the US. As crayon historian John W. Kropf notes, "The movement promoted the idea of developing the whole child, which included creative expression. Numerous companies sought to fill this demand and entered the market, offering various types of wax crayons."

Crayons enter American classrooms in the 1880s, and purple has always been one of the colors in the box. In its first box of Crayola crayons (eight colors, 1903), Binney & Smith—which would become the dominant brand by 1910—included a purple. Crayola became the leader in crayons, in part, because the company's leaders—Edwin Binney and Harold Smith—understood children as their primary market, and so made their crayons with non-toxic materials. Though some colors could be developed from ground rocks and minerals, Crayola made purple via chemically blended pigments and clays that were hand-stirred, "poured into crayon-shaped molds designed for children's hands, and then cooled and hardened."

In the early days of Crayola, the purple crayon's *name* varied. It was sometimes called *violet*, even though violet and purple are different colors—violet occupying a unique place at the end of the color spectrum and purple a combination of red and blue. During Johnson's childhood, Crayola used the names interchangeably.[1] Whatever the color was called, Johnson would have had access to purple crayons as a young boy, both in the schoolroom and out—by 1912, crayon manufacturers were selling their product in penny-packages. That would be about 25¢ in today's dollars. In choosing a purple crayon, Johnson seems to be recalling his own childhood drawing.

14

Color, Part I

Why These Four?

But he's not choosing his favorite color, brown. He reserved brown for Harold's outline, the type, the cover, and much of his own daily life. He drove a brown 1948 Austin Tudor sedan, lived in a brown house, and always wore brown: chocolate-colored pants and T-shirts, brown cardigan sweaters, or (if obliged to wear formal attire) a brown suit. Johnson's sartorial minimalism echoes Harold's aesthetic and solves the practical daily question of what to wear: brown goes with brown. Indeed, brown marks the boundaries of both Johnson's body and Harold's. The clear brown line offers the boy artist's body a definition that is both crisp and soft. It is as firm as a black boundary, but not quite as hard.

From an aesthetic perspective, the combination of brown and purple is about the relationship between the two colors. Brown is warm, purple is bright. A full page of brown would darken the mood; a page of solid purple would assault our eyes. The dominant color (the white background) creates a gentle intimacy, drawing us in; the small volume of purple and of brown maintains a quiet balance, brown subtly grounding Harold, and purple lighting his way forward. It's also worth noting that, since purple is red plus blue, and brown is red plus yellow plus black, the colors' shared ingredient—red—gently underscores the fact that that the purple crayon is an extension of brown Harold.

However, perhaps that's too simple an explanation. As Josef Albers points out in his influential *Interaction of Color* (1961), *all* colors are connected and related to *all* other colors, and "any color

How to Draw the World: Harold and the Purple Crayon *and the Making of a Children's Classic.* Philip Nel, Oxford University Press. © Oxford University Press 2024. DOI: 10.1093/oso/9780197777596.003.0015

Figure 16. Crockett Johnson, original cover art, *Harold and the Purple Crayon*. Image courtesy of the Smithsonian Institution. Reproduced courtesy of The Ruth Krauss Foundation, Inc.

'goes' or 'works' with any other color, presupposing that their quantities are appropriate." As Albers says, no "mechanical color system" fully explains the relationship between quantity, form, recurrence, and the many "changing factors" that emerge when we put theory into practice: "Good painting, good coloring, is comparable to good cooking. Even a good cooking recipe demands tasting and repeated tasting while it is being followed. And the best tasting still depends on a cook with taste."

A master chef in this regard, Johnson understood that color is about relationships, allowing him to create nighttime on a white page. Though all but one of the Harold books take place in the evening, only in *Harold's Trip to the Sky* does Johnson give us black (well, dark brown) pages, and then only during the period when Harold enters the darkness of outer space. The dark backgrounds of *Harold's Trip to the Sky* make the book's dangers—the Martian "thing" in the flying saucer, for instance—feel a bit more dangerous. In contrast, light backgrounds also lighten the mood.

As Molly Bang puts it, "White or light backgrounds feel safer to us than dark backgrounds because we can see well during the day and only poorly at night." Also: a purple crayon "pops" on a white background but lacks such sharp contrast on a black one. In *Harold and the Purple Crayon*, we read these light backgrounds as night because the narrator twice mentions Harold's "walk in the moonlight," and Harold confirms this claim by providing a moon. As in the theatre, language and props create reality. A lantern indicates night on stage, and a moon conveys night on the page. In the audience, watching Harold's play unfold, we accept the reality that Johnson and his protagonist create for us. White becomes night.

15

Narrative & Perspective

Here's another curiosity that you may not have noticed but that, when you do notice it, is hard to ignore. Early in the book, Harold "left the path for a short cut across a field." But what does the phrase "short cut" mean when you're creating your own world? Since physical space is empty (save for our trio of Harold, crayon, and moon), the line of Harold's imagination can take us or him anywhere. Johnson's use of the phrase "short cut"—twice, once on each of two consecutive pages—creates a kind of free indirect discourse (or "*style indirect libre*"), inviting readers to adopt Harold's perspective. In voicing Harold's thoughts, apparently as Harold is in the process of having these thoughts, Johnson's narrator creates an emotional intimacy between reader and boy. He invites us to imagine Harold imagining. This is "right where a forest ought to be," which inspires Harold to draw a tree, though only one so he "doesn't get lost in the woods," echoing his earlier idea of drawing "a long straight path so he wouldn't get lost." A very practical approach to art and navigation.

However, I call this narration a "kind of" free indirect discourse because, although it offers Harold's first-person point of view via third-person sentences, its diction and perspective also exceed that of our 3-year-old protagonist—who, incidentally, speaks in only *one* of the seven *Harold* books. I expect that Johnson usually keeps Harold silent so that he can create a narration that aligns itself *both* with Harold *and* with an older, more sophisticated reader. The claim "he made a small forest, with just one tree in it" may be perfectly logical to a 3-year-old, but comically absurd to older readers who know that a forest requires more than a single tree.

How to Draw the World: Harold and the Purple Crayon *and the Making of a Children's Classic.* Philip Nel, Oxford University Press. © Oxford University Press 2024. DOI: 10.1093/oso/9780197777596.003.0016

16

Humor

The tension between these points of view is the source of much of the books' humor. As Kant wrote in *The Critique of Pure Judgment*, laughter arises from incongruity—"the sudden transformation of a strained expectation into nothing." Comparing music to laughter, he says that both arise from "different kinds of play with aesthetical ideas,…which can give lively gratification merely by their changes." Johnson's play frequently arrives via language that oscillates between adults' and children's perspectives or that gestures in more than one direction (puns, double meanings). Though always delivered in a gentle tone (Johnson never seems to be mocking Harold), the book's puns and other jokes require some linguistic sophistication. When Harold "was over his head in an ocean," Johnson means the phrase "over his head" literally (Harold is truly sinking here) and figuratively (Harold is in trouble). Similarly, he "came up thinking fast" conveys the literal sense of coming up out of the water and the figurative one of coming up with an idea. He "made land without much trouble" suggests both the act of mooring his boat on the shore *and* of drawing—or making—the land where he docks his boat. Given that the *Harold* books' central conceit is visual, it's surprising how many of Johnson's jokes are verbal.

There is visual humor in the *Harold* books—the goggle-eyed policeman in *Harold and the Purple Crayon* or the moment when what looks like a flying saucer turns out to be an oatmeal bowl in *Harold's Trip to the Sky*. But pictorial comedic scenes are rare. I suspect humor emerges less in the books' art because, throughout his work, Crockett Johnson almost never indulges in the

How to Draw the World: Harold and the Purple Crayon and the Making of a Children's Classic. Philip Nel, Oxford University Press. © Oxford University Press 2024. DOI: 10.1093/oso/9780197777596.003.0017

exaggerations of visual caricature. With the complicated exception of Howard the Sigahstaw Indian (who appears in eighteen *Barnaby* strips in the fall of 1945),[1] Johnson avoided amplifying perceived national or racial differences—in contrast to his contemporary, Dr. Seuss, who trafficked in caricature in both his political cartoons and his children's books. The most striking moment of visual outrageousness in the *Harold* books—the clown in *Harold's Circus*—feels like Johnson thinking in a different, broader comic style because that is exactly what he is doing. He's aligning the art with Harold's perspective. The clown's bulbous nose, too-long shoes, and lunging Groucho-Marx stride all make Harold laugh. Though it is the sole moment in the seven books where Harold laughs, the scene represents not Johnson's sense of humor but rather how Harold understands the humor of circus clowns. Drawing the clown so that he can cover up an accidentally "ridiculous somersault," Harold "pretended he had been clowning. He quickly put on a clown's hat. He put on a clown's smile on his face." Just as Harold "acted silly, like a clown," so too Johnson's art is "putting on" clownishness, sympathetically rendering Harold's play.

Figure 17. Crockett Johnson laughing, 1967. Photograph by Nina Stagakis.

On writing humor for young people, Johnson said, "Humor for children must be written for adults. I cannot think of a good humorous children's book that has not been. An inconsistency or a line or situation that makes a grownup wince is almost certain to insult, or worse, bore a child." Though this approach surely results in the youngest readers missing some of the *Harold* books' humor, enjoying the books does not depend upon readers getting the joke. You can still follow the plot and enjoy *Harold's Trip to the Sky* if you miss the fact that "drew up a chair" refers both to the crayon's creation of a chair and to Harold bringing a chair closer to him. There's only one moment in the books in which Johnson glances toward the more sophisticated satire of his *Barnaby* comic: Harold's recollection, in the same book, of "how the government has fun on the desert. It shoots off rockets." An older reader in 1957 might see this as a sly comment on the accelerating "space race" between the US and USSR, but younger ones could understand it as literally true without feeling that the narrator were talking over their heads. In the late 1950s, the US government *did* like to shoot off rockets. So, why shouldn't Harold?

The idiosyncrasies of a child's logic, another recurring source of humor in the books, is also never delivered in a way that invites laughter *at* young people. Harold creates "a nice simple picnic lunch." Turn the page, and the unexpected "There was nothing but pie" is the punch-line. On the next page, "But there were all nine kinds of pie that Harold liked best" extends the logic of the joke. The notion of a "simple picnic lunch" containing "nothing but pie" is funny. But it is also a delicious fantasy. If parents might chuckle at Harold's indifference to nutrition, most children would welcome their nine favorite kinds of pie. Similarly, an older reader might smile at the idea of finding your bedroom by drawing its window around the moon. But, from Harold's perspective, it's an ingenious solution.

17

Windows, Part II

The View from Johnson's Desk

From the window above the desk where he wrote *Harold*, Crockett Johnson could see his boat, moored at the dock across the street. He also saw the front yard, a fence, Rowayton Avenue, as well as (to Johnson's right) trees, and (to Johnson's left) the Five Mile River just before it entered Long Island Sound, on its way to the ocean. Since ocean, boat, road, tree, and front yard all appear in *Harold and the Purple Crayon*, I suspect Johnson's location influenced Harold's adventures.

In September 2014, I stood in that very room, enjoying the afternoon light streaming through the house's many windows—abundant windows are another connection between Johnson's book and his home. I was in town to give an evening talk on Johnson and Krauss to the Rowayton Historical Society, and the owners of 74 Rowayton Avenue kindly invited me to visit their home. Thanks to a floorplan sketched from memory by Nina Stagakis (about whom, more in Chapter 19), I was able to see exactly where Johnson sat while creating the dummies for *Harold and the Purple Crayon*. Looking out that front window, I thought not only of the overlap between what Johnson saw and what he drew, but between past and present, between what is gone and what remains.

In architecture's capacity to acknowledge history and the passage of time, the experience of being in the house was in some ways the opposite of immersing oneself in a *Harold* book. The house's physical presence creates a context in which to imagine its

How to Draw the World: Harold and the Purple Crayon *and the Making of a Children's Classic.* Philip Nel, Oxford University Press. © Oxford University Press 2024. DOI: 10.1093/oso/9780197777596.003.0018

Figure 18. Crockett Johnson and Ruth Krauss, front porch of their Rowayton home, 1959. Image courtesy of the Smithsonian Institution. Reproduced courtesy of the *New Haven Register*.

former residents, but the blank page lacks context, nothing to jog a memory or attempt to correlate with a photo. On the page, Harold's purple minimalism offers enough specificity to distinguish between things (we can tell a moose from a porcupine, a pie from the moon) but not enough to endow them with realistic

Figure 19. Same front porch, 2014. Photo by Philip Nel.

specificity (though there are nine kinds of pie, all of Harold's pies look alike). On the abstraction-to-realism scale, Harold's iconic style is closer to the pictographic language of the cartoon and farther from the vividly realistic detail of a Vermeer painting or a Van Allsburg picture book. Particularity activates memory and, in my visit, activated only *imagined* memory, conjured via Nina's floor-plan and via photographs of Johnson and Krauss in their home in the 1950s and 1960s.

The place was and was not as it had been in Johnson's day. His clear view of the river was then partially obscured by construction. His office had become a dining room, and his dining room had become a living room. Yet, this was still the house where he and Krauss lived for twenty-seven years. As past and present mingled, I recalled Richard McGuire's innovative six-page comic, "Here" (1989), which would be published in a book-length version three months after my visit. Exploring comics' ability to spatialize time, "Here" presents many moments simultaneously—all taking place in the space occupied by a single room. Reading the comic (and, later, the book), you piece together some of the lives of those who passed through that space. In the process, you experience just how temporal—and temporary—any "here" is.

18

Time

Though it lacks *Here*'s extended meditation on the subject, *Harold and the Purple Crayon* also takes us on a journey through time. The word appears in the first sentence of the story: "One evening, after thinking it over for some time…," Harold decides on his walk in the moonlight. Conveying an awareness of time's passage, the narrative offers many temporal markers: the moon, moonlight, "in no time he was climbing aboard a trim little boat," making land "[a]fter he had sailed long enough," Harold's memory of picnics (the past), and an awareness of bedtime—first indicated by Harold feeling "tired" and thinking that "he ought to be getting to bed."

But how much time passes? What is the duration of Harold's adventure?

If we measure a story's duration by how long it takes to read, the pace will vary. After writing the previous sentence, I timed myself reading *Harold and the Purple Crayon* aloud. It took me 4 minutes and 53 seconds. There are no recordings of Crockett Johnson reading the book, but he had a slow, deliberate speaking style: his reading time would be longer than mine. Reading *Harold* might take you more time or less time. You might dwell longer on certain pictures or pause to answer questions from a young listener. If especially tired, listener or reader might drop off to sleep before Harold does. All of these will alter the amount of time spent.

If the story is a dream (which, as Chapter 27 explores, it may be), then it might take anywhere from a few seconds to a half hour to a full 90 minutes of Rapid-Eye-Movement (REM) sleep, when most dreaming occurs. (Ninety minutes is the typical amount of

REM for 7–8 hours of sleep.) If the story is not a dream, then it seems to take place in a single evening. Unlike the moon in *Where the Wild Things Are*, the moon in *Harold and the Purple Crayon* never changes phase, though its position in the sky does change. These details suggest that the adventure takes place during one night.

That said, these methods—measuring length of dream or of read-aloud—assume that time is a property of clocks or wrist-watches. However, as Alan Burdick's *Why Time Flies* points out, "Time is a property of the mind." Or, to borrow Simone de Beauvoir's words, "The way in which we experience the day-to-day flow of time depends on what it holds."

So, how Harold experiences time would depend very much upon what he is doing. Drawing the city full of windows must take far longer than drawing his bedroom window. But emotional experience also shapes temporal experience. When he is fully absorbed in drawing his city, Harold may not notice time passing at all. The more deeply engaged we are in a task, the more time seems to disappear.

Safety or its absence also affects time. If we fall from a danger-ous height (as Harold does), time seems to slow down. Under extreme stress, our senses are more alert, and we perceive more within a shorter period of clock time. As a result, time seems to slip into a slow-motion languor. Lewis Carroll's *Alice's Adventures in Wonderland* registers this experience in chapter 1, as Alice falls:

> The rabbit-hole went straight on like a tunnel for some way, and then dipped suddenly down, so suddenly that Alice had not a moment to think about stopping herself before she found herself falling down a very deep well.
>
> Either the well was very deep, or she fell very slowly, for she had plenty of time as she went down to look about her and to wonder what was going to happen next.

On the "falling, in thin air" pages, Johnson conveys this sensation by removing those visual referents that might otherwise anchor Harold in a particular moment. The blankness of the page also heightens our awareness of Harold's peril by focusing the attention on Harold himself—a human child tumbling through space. If a reader identifies with Harold, then the reader's experience of time may also slacken or quicken according to how perilous Harold's journey feels to them.

That said, since time passes more quickly for adults than it does for children, an adult and a child looking at the same copy of *Harold and the Purple Crayon* simultaneously would not have the same temporal experience of Harold's adventure. As Burdick points out, time may feel quicker for adults because we remember more of the past and less of the present: "When we're young virtually every experience is new, so it remains vivid years later. But as we age, habit and routine become the norm; novel experiences are fewer (we've done everything already) and we barely take notice of the time we currently inhabit." Or it may be that, as adults, time's pace simply worries us more, since we have less time left.

I think that the change in ratio of one's age to a unit of time is the main reason that the experience of childhood, as it happens, feels longer than the experience of adulthood, as it happens. As Burdick reports, philosopher Paul Janet even came up with a formula to explain the sensation of time speeding up as we age: "The apparent length of a given span of time varies inversely in proportion to your age. One year seems five times shorter to a fifty-year-old man than to a ten-year-old boy, because a year is one-fiftieth of the man's life and only one tenth of the boy's." I don't know whether Johnson knew this formula, though I am sure that he would have enjoyed it. An amateur mathematician himself, he was also then a 48-year-old man imagining a 3-year-old child's adventures and borrowing the kid's crayon to draw them.

19

The Real Harolds

The book's narrative voice sounds like both adult and child. However, thinking in terms of an adult-child dichotomy imposes an artificial boundary, effacing the many voices—adults' and children's—that shape the book's unique perspective. As scholar Marah Gubar reminds us, "Children and adults are separated by differences of degree, not of kind.... Our younger and older selves are multiple and interlinked, akin to one another rather than wholly distinct." Harold combines the selves of at least one adult and three children. The adult is Johnson himself. That one-tree forest that I earlier described as "comically absurd" to adults, was not *only* that to him. For an artist who claimed (as Johnson did) that he didn't like to draw, a one-tree forest is efficient metonymy—letting the part stand for the whole. As a child, he actually did love to draw, and so one of the children behind Harold is *also* Johnson. That Harold combines both 8-year-old and 48-year-old Johnson also represents adult Johnson's insight that there's *not* a fundamental division between "adult" and "child"—that, as he told a journalist in 1959, adults and small children are amused by the same things. "Teen-agers are different, but as you get older you sort of revert to your childhood," he said.

The teenager he knew best when he spoke those words was Nina Rowand Wallace, who—when he wrote *Harold and the Purple Crayon*—was his 8-year-old office mate. In September 1954, a car accident killed her dad, Johnson's friend Gene Wallace. Afterward, Nina's mother Phyllis Rowand (an artist who illustrated three books by Ruth Krauss) and Nina began spending a lot

How to Draw the World: Harold and the Purple Crayon *and the Making of a Children's Classic.* Philip Nel, Oxford University Press. © Oxford University Press 2024. DOI: 10.1093/oso/9780197777596.003.0020

Figure 20. David "Crockett" Johnson Leisk as a boy, with his mother Mary Leisk. Photo courtesy of the Smithsonian Institution.

more time with Johnson and Krauss, often having dinner at their house. Johnson even built Nina a Nina-sized desk in *his* office. While she sat and drew at her desk, he might sit and draw *Harold and the Purple Crayon* at his. Nina was the child to whom he was closest, the daughter he never had. (He and Krauss were childless.)

The third child behind the fictional Harold is Harold Frank, Johnson's nephew. Johnson's mother's death, in 1953, had brought Johnson temporarily closer to his sister, Else Frank. When Johnson finished the book's dummy in November of 1954, he named the protagonist after his sister's nearly 2-year-old son whom she had adopted the previous year—naming the lad for Harold Gold, the attorney who helped with the adoption. Perhaps readers who are saddened by the predicament of Johnson's protagonist—such as journalist Chris Mautner, who notes that Harold is "utterly alone

Figure 21. Nina Rowand Wallace, age 4. Photo by Agnes Goodman. Courtesy of Nina Stagakis.

Figure 22. Harold Frank, age 2. Photo courtesy of Harold Frank.

except for whatever he willed into being"—are sensing a melancholic, autobiographical subtext of departed parents (Johnson's, Nina's) and of children needing care (Nina, Harold). Or they may be responding to the many real dangers that Harold faces, the first of which is nearly drowning.

20

Metapictures

The near-drowning happens when the dragon guarding the apple tree in Harold's one-tree forest frightens Harold, who backs away, and "His hand holding the purple crayon shook." The shaking crayon draws a wavy scribble that can be read in at least three ways: (1) the expected result of a shaky crayon, (2) a series of carefully conjoined cursive *w*'s, and (3) the surface of an ocean in the visual language of the comic strip. The text encourages us to read the image as *ocean*, but it never quite loses its senses of wobbly *w*'s nor of errant crayon. It's like the duck/rabbit or face/vase metapicture, *even though* Johnson's narrative guides us to resolve the competing interpretations into a single one—an ocean.

This ocean line is but one of the double images in *Harold and the Purple Crayon*. Harold draws a shape, which at first is abstract or geometrical, and then—guided by Johnson's text and Harold's additions—becomes something particular. A balloon begins as the arc of a circle. Rectangles become windows, repeated windows make buildings, and many buildings are a city. That Johnson makes this carefully planned journey seem improvised by a small child is what makes *Harold and the Purple Crayon* a work of genius.

How to Draw the World: Harold and the Purple Crayon *and the Making of a Children's Classic.* Philip Nel, Oxford University Press. © Oxford University Press 2024. DOI: 10.1093/oso/9780197777596.003.0021

**Welche Thiere gleichen ein=
ander am meisten?**

Kaninchen und Ente.

Figure 23. "Rabbit and Duck" ("Kaninchen und Ente"), as it appeared in the weekly Munich humor magazine *Fliegende Blätter* on October 23, 1892. The caption asks, "Which animals resemble each other most?" The following month, the "Rabbit and Duck" illustration appeared *without* the caption in the US magazine *Harper's Weekly*. It would become a favorite of psychologists and philosophers—notably, Ludwig Wittgenstein, whose *Philosophical Investigations* was in 1953 simultaneously published both in its original German (*Philosophischen Untersuchungen*) and in G. E. M. Anscombe's English translation.

21

The Big Picture

I'm not exaggerating when I call Johnson a genius. He thinks and draws with the precision of a mathematician because he *was* an amateur mathematician who published two theorems of his own and devoted the last decade of his life to geometric paintings of theorems—a motif I see in the rhombus that makes up the kite (in *Harold's ABC*) and the circle of Harold's hot-air balloon. (One of Johnson's original theorems involved squaring the circle, the painting version of which is the sixth image in the color insert.) A one-time student of typographer Fredric Goudy and a magazine art editor for over a decade, Johnson had a keen sense of layout and design. Only someone with his sharp attention to detail could write a book that is actually one giant drawing, revealed one page at a time. Harold does not erase. His crayon lines solidify into a reality he is both navigating and making. To suggest that this precise, carefully laid-out landscape is all Harold's spontaneous creation, Johnson must have mapped it all out in advance, and then decided which moments to reveal on each page.

During the process of animating *Harold's Fairy Tale*, Gene Deitch put it this way, in a letter to Johnson: "Each of these [Harold] stories is as precisely constructed as any of your mathematical paintings....At first sight, they may seem simple to some people, but anyone who gets involved with their structure will soon find how intricately they are built." Three years earlier, Deitch's work animating *A Picture for Harold's Room* showed him this intricacy. Working at his Prague studio, Deitch had been sending Johnson (in Connecticut) ideas for adapting the book as an animated cartoon. Initially, Deitch included "cinematic

How to Draw the World: Harold and the Purple Crayon *and the Making of a Children's Classic.* Philip Nel, Oxford University Press. © Oxford University Press 2024. DOI: 10.1093/oso/9780197777596.003.0022

Figure 24. Crockett Johnson and a version of his *Squared Circle*,
c. 1972. Photo by Jackie Curtis.

close-ups, camera move-ins, and cuts." Johnson called it "the worst
storyboard" he'd ever seen. Via a series of postcards, he helped
Deitch understand that for the film to work on the screen, Harold
must be (in Deitch's words) "the exact same size in relation to the
film frame," and that "the entire film must appear to be one continuous scene."

One other challenge: if they filmed Harold by adding a little bit
of his line with each shot, the line would appear wiggly "which
would destroy the illusion that Harold is really making a drawing
with his purple crayon." To get a smooth line, they would have to
shoot backwards. So, Deitch and his assistants created Harold's
entire drawing first. Then, they shot the film. Placing 7,500 different drawings of Harold (one at a time, in reverse order) over this
landscape, they had him "undraw" the scenery, erasing the entire
picture, one tiny increment at a time. Only when they projected

the film forward did the picture reappear. It was, Deitch said, "Just about the most difficult film we ever made here, and exactly <u>because</u> it looks so simple!" With "no cuts, no zooms, and no backgrounds, [...] nothing can be hidden. It must be smooth and perfect." Re-read through the process of animated adaptation, these books' complexities come into sharper focus. Johnson's *Harold* books are so meticulously designed that the films could only deliver the magic of Harold's crayon by animating in reverse.

22

Where and When Is Harold?

Deitch created those two films in the early 1970s, but Johnson wrote *Harold and the Purple Crayon* in 1954. If you didn't see the 1955 date on the copyright page, could you have guessed that? To borrow one of my favorite questions from picture-book scholar Perry Nodelman's close-reading of John Burningham's *Mr. Gumpy's Outing* (in an essay that partly inspired this book): *About what facts is the book silent?* Much of what I've written addresses facets of this question, but *Harold and the Purple Crayon* is especially silent about its historical moment. We know that Harold's is a world with sailboats and oceans, mountains and hot-air balloons, helpful policemen and tall buildings.

But Harold's iconic artistic style (which is nearly but not *quite* identical to Johnson's iconic artistic style) effaces the specific details that would allow us to date the events in the book. The policeman's uniform—a cap and a smock with a giant star—betrays little about when or where it might have been worn. The buildings in Harold's "city full of windows" lack architectural particularity. They date to the era of the skyscraper, but that's a wide window of time, starting in the 1880s and continuing to the present day. The streamlined style makes them look more modern (post-1950), but, since Harold's minimalism effaces details, it's hard to know whether their apparent modernity is a result of Harold's artistic style or of the buildings' architectural style. And which city is this? It has many skyscrapers close together which narrows down the possible cities. New York, Chicago, and Tokyo would be more likely than Washington or Rome. Johnson offers sufficient specificity to provide a sense of place but not enough to

How to Draw the World: Harold and the Purple Crayon *and the Making of a Children's Classic*. Philip Nel, Oxford University Press. © Oxford University Press 2024. DOI: 10.1093/oso/9780197777596.003.0023

identify *which* place, or *when*. Only the copyright date—1955—indicates that the place is most likely New York because it then had more skyscrapers than any other city.

The artwork's iconic ambiguity explains, in part, the book's appeal to such a broad range of readers. To borrow Scott McCloud's ideas, the more iconic an image is, the more universal it seems. When a character lacks clearly defined facial features, readers project themselves onto the character, filling in the details—in this case, identifying with a crayon-wielding child. McCloud calls this principle "amplification through simplification." Harold is also something of a cipher, a mere conduit for the purple crayon. Though his name is masculine, his behavior does little to "gender" him as a character: he exhibits traits that are stereotypically masculine (an adventurous spirit, climbing mountains) and stereotypically feminine (such as his thoughtfulness in sharing the pie or common sense in asking for directions). And he wears a white unisex onesie.

23

Cute!

Also known as footie pajamas, his outfit aligns Harold with the *cute*. An American aesthetic judgment and style that emerges in the nineteenth century, cuteness typically entails smallness, roundness, and softness—all features of Harold's appearance. Precociousness, another element of the cute, also sometimes appears in the *Harold* books. As Daniel Harris observes, we find it cute when children mimic us grown-ups, a mimicry Harold performs in catering a pie-themed picnic lunch, trying to banish mosquitos with smoke (in *Harold's Fairy Tale*) and shooting off rockets (in *Harold's Trip to the Sky*). What makes these actions cute is that they are not entirely successful imitations. As Lori Merish says of Shirley Temple, "Her precocity both instates her resemblance to adults and her critical difference from them." Harold's imitative behaviors are cutest when they fall short, reminding us of his difference.

Yet the adjective "cute" is less frequently applied to Harold than you might think. My students sometimes call Harold "cute," as do a small minority of reviews on Goodreads and Amazon. Contemporary reviews of the *Harold* books did not call ether the stories or the character "cute." Some, however, did adopt cute-adjacent language. According to reviewers in the 1950s, Harold is an "adventurous moppet," an "ingenious moppet," a "delightful small scamp," a "saucer-eyed little boy," or a "saucer-eyed small boy." All of this language evokes elements of the cute. They focus on his large eyes, diminutive size ("small," "little," "moppet"), and precocity ("ingenious moppet").

How to Draw the World: Harold and the Purple Crayon *and the Making of a Children's Classic.* Philip Nel, Oxford University Press. © Oxford University Press 2024. DOI: 10.1093/oso/9780197777596.003.0024

The tone of both "ingenious moppet" and "delightful small scamp" also conveys playful judgment and figure Harold as an inherently vulnerable figure. To paraphrase Sianne Ngai and Gérard Genette, these descriptors—like the term *cute* itself—conceal their judgment beneath the pretense of describing. They also underscore that, as Ngai argues, "all aesthetic judgments...are really...demands." Yet, if these reviewers insist on Harold's cuteness, both Harold and Johnson also resist their demands.

Cuteness is both form and feeling. The Harold books display elements of cute style, but do not invite the expected emotional response to cuteness. They do not inspire an *awwww*. As Ngai writes, "Resulting in a squeal or a cluck, a murmur or a coo, the cute object seems to have the power to infantilize the language of its infantalizer." The cute also asks for our care, solicits our cuddles, needs our help and, as Ngai puts it, "seems to want us and only us as its mommy." If dressing him in his jammies conveys any sense that Harold is vulnerable or requires our assistance, he quickly corrects that impression. He is resourceful, creative, adept at solving his own problems. In this sense, he is quite the opposite of the modern sense of *cute*, instead embodying an older meaning and the direct ancestor of *cute*: *acute*. Ngai again: "'Cute' derives from the older 'acute' in a process linguists call aphaeresis (the process by which words lose initial unstressed syllables to generate shorter and 'cuter' versions of themselves; 'alone' becomes 'lone,' 'until' becomes 'til')." And Harold is acute: keen, quick-witted, mentally alert.

An acute thinker himself, Johnson seems dispositionally suspicious of the modern *cute*. In *The Blue Ribbon Puppies* (1958), a picture book that marks his sole extended foray into the *awwww* cute, he transforms the aesthetic's expected affect into a punch line. A little boy and a little girl decide to award a blue ribbon to the best of their seven pups. On the first page, "They tried a ribbon on one pup. 'He is too fat,' said the boy." Turn the page, and

There were seven pups, and the
children said, "We will put a blue
ribbon on the BEST puppy here."
They tried a ribbon on one pup.
"He is too fat," said the boy.

Figure 25. Crockett Johnson, *The Blue Ribbon Puppies* (1958),
pp. 2–3. Reproduced courtesy of The Ruth Krauss Foundation, Inc.

"The puppy looked at him." In response to the pup's cuteness,
"'He's the best,' the boy said. 'the best FAT puppy.'" That pattern
then repeats six more times. The two children find that each
pup—whether fat, spotty, long, tall, small, shaggy, or plain—is
quite remarkable in his own cute way. So, they give each a ribbon.
At the book's conclusion, Johnson undercuts the image of the puppies as adorable, malleable playmates. The final page shows only
the debris of the blue ribbons—the puppies and the children having since departed. Johnson's ending asserts the puppies' autonomy and offers a gentle laugh at the infantilizing myth of cuteness.

Rather than save his "reveal" for the end of a *Harold* book,
Johnson throughout affirms his protagonist's autonomy and
sharpness of mind. Harold's eyes have the perfect roundness of
cute eyes, but there's no supplicating glance in our direction.
Unlike Rose O'Neill's Kewpies or the children and puppies in *The
Blue Ribbon Puppies*, we never see both of Harold's eyes at once.

Johnson shows him only from the side, eyes looking ahead, as he charts his course.

There's one other key difference between Harold and the dominant idea of *cute* in the 1950s. Then, cuteness was white. But Harold is not.

24

Color, Part II

Is Harold Black?

If your response to the previous sentence is some version of "Wrong! Harold is a little white boy," I quite understand. When I was a little white boy, I too read him as white. The designers who created the current HarperCollins cover also saw Harold that way: in 1998, they changed his original tan complexion to light peach. Their decision likely influenced the creators of the *Harold and the Purple Crayon* TV show (HBO, 2001–2002) and the *Harold and the Purple Crayon* iPad app (2011) to use similar colors for Harold's skin tone, encouraging more people to see him as a white child. The 1998 change to the covers of the *Harold* books has made Harold's whiteness canon.

But not everyone has seen Harold as white—possibly, not even Johnson himself. When cartoonist Chris Ware was a little white boy, he read Harold as "black," his "tawny skin (the only tint in the entire series)," and when she was a little white girl, novelist Mairead Case saw "Harold's skin" as "slightly tinted": "The baby-sitter who first read him to me said he was black, and so I identified him that way for a long time." When he was a little Black boy, picture book creator Bryan Collier both read Harold as Black and "imagined himself as Harold." Collier, Ware and Case's babysitter all have a point. As the book's mechanicals reveal, Harold's skin color *is* "10% BROWN." So. Given that Johnson gave him a light brown complexion, should we read Harold as a child of color? Here are three answers to that question.

How to Draw the World: Harold and the Purple Crayon *and the Making of a Children's Classic.* Philip Nel, Oxford University Press. © Oxford University Press 2024. DOI: 10.1093/oso/9780197777596.003.0025

First, one reason that Harold's skin is 10 percent brown may be cost. Unlike other picture books at the time, which might have used three or four colors, *Harold and the Purple Crayon* used only two: brown and purple. The offset color lithography printing process required that the color be added in two phases: a purple phase (C4) and a brown phase (C3). The "(PURPLE)" and "(BROWN)" on the mechanicals are instructions to the printer. "10% BROWN" tells the printer to use a screen (over Harold's face and hands) that filters out all but 10 percent of the brown color. Using tiny dots scaled to 10 percent, the printer inks solid brown over 10 percent of the area; combined with the white page, 10 percent brown creates Harold's tan skin.

So, Collier, Ware and Case's babysitter have correctly identified the hue of Harold's pigmentation. That said, skin color is not race. And it's quite possible that Johnson was restricting himself to just two colors to keep costs down.

However, as cartoonist and comics historian Mark Newgarden pointed out to me, using 10 percent brown to create "Caucasian 'flesh'" is rather unusual. In the ubiquitous mass-media 4-color cartoon context of the day, racially white skin would have been created with a magenta screen. Within Johnson's two-color printing plan, Newgarden says, "paper stock white and 10% of that purple (close to pink) are both visually closer to how Caucasian 'flesh' would typically be represented" at that time (C7). So, he suggests, "brown was deliberate—at least within that self-imposed set of options."

The rarity of using 10 percent brown suggests a second possible reading. Making a child of color the central character of his Harold books, Crockett Johnson was at the vanguard of mainstream American children's literature: he was creating an African American protagonist nine years before Ezra Jack Keats's *The Snowy Day* (1962) would become the first book featuring a Black protagonist to win the Caldecott Medal. That may have been his intent. Johnson had been publicly pro-Civil Rights since the

1940s. In a 1940 political cartoon published six weeks before the classic white-supremacist film *Gone with the Wind* (1939) won eight Oscars, Johnson satirizes that movie's racist propaganda. When in 1944 the National Committee to Abolish the Poll Tax asked if it could use his *Barnaby* strips in its campaign, he agreed—*Barnaby* has a three-strip sequence skewering the racist tax. In 1945, Johnson signed on to the End Jim Crow in Baseball Committee and the Committee for Equal Justice for Mrs. Recy Taylor. That same year, Johnson supported the reelection of Ben Davis, the radical Black politician who represented Harlem on the New York City Council from 1943 to 1949.

Six months before he sent *Harold and the Purple Crayon* to Ursula Nordstrom, the US Supreme Court's *Brown vs. Board of Education* decision ruled that "separate educational facilities are inherently unequal"—which, many people thought at the time, would end school segregation. (It didn't.) A few years earlier, Nordstrom had rejected Ruth Krauss's attempts at writing an anti-racist children's book, but Krauss and Maurice Sendak managed to smuggle in a message of racial equality into their *I Want to Paint My Bathroom Blue*. The "house like a rainbow" scene, in which Sendak draws the child's friends in a rainbow of colors (yellow, pink, blue, brown, purple) was, Krauss said, "a definite statement in 'race' integration." Though the book was not published until 1956, they were working on it at the Johnson-Krauss home while Johnson was working on Harold. Perhaps their efforts inspired him to make a comparably subtle political statement by coloring Harold tan.

If that were the case, then what do we make of contemporary reviewers' failure to note Krauss and Sendak's pro-integration message, or to comment upon the brownness of Harold's skin? Did excessive subtlety prevent a theme of racial inclusiveness from reaching the audiences of *Harold and the Purple Crayon* and *I Want to Paint My Bathroom Blue*? My answer—and a third answer to the question of whether to read Harold as Black or Brown—is that ambiguity can be politically useful. I don't know whether Johnson intended to make a pro-Civil Rights statement, but Harold's coloring allows him to be read as more than one race. Since advocates of racial equality in the 1950s risked being censured as "Communist," the subtlety of 10 percent brown grants Johnson and his publisher political cover. It's subtle enough that book reviewers might fail to notice it. However, a few adult reviewers are hardly a representative sample of the eager readership of a book that, within a month of its publication, sold out its initial print run of 10,000 copies, and had its publisher ordering a new print run of seventy-five hundred more. Some of those thousands of readers *did* see Harold as Black.

Racial ambiguity makes it easier for readers of any race to identify with Harold. I don't know whether future musical genius Prince or future US Poet Laureate Rita Dove read Harold as a child of color, but, when they were children, both artists saw themselves in Harold. Dove, 3 years old at the time of the book's publication, said that *Harold and the Purple Crayon* was her first favorite book because "it showed me the possibilities of traveling along the line of one's imagination," an idea that made a "powerful impression" on her—so powerful that it appears in her poem "Maple Valley Branch Library, 1967." In it, she writes of being able to "take / the path of Harold's purple crayon through / the bedroom window and onto a lavender / spill of stars."

Unless "I only want to see you underneath the purple rain" (in "Purple Rain") alludes to Harold standing underneath the purple rain in *Harold's Fairy Tale*, Prince's lyrics make no specific references to Johnson's *Harold* books. But *Harold and the Purple Crayon* was Prince's favorite childhood book and is the reason he adopted the color purple. As Mattie Shaw, Prince's mother, told biographer Neal Karlen, "Prince loved 'pretend.' And his favorite book was *Harold and the Purple Crayon*. You remember that book? It was his favorite book ever since John [Nelson, Prince's father] took him to work one day at Honeywell and told Prince what he really did for a living at Honeywell—the child must have been six or seven, it was one of those 'take your kids to work days' they used to have."[1] Linking *Harold* with "pretend" and with Prince's father—a Honeywell plastics molder and jazz pianist who named his son after his stage name, "Prince Rogers"—suggests that Prince strongly identified with Harold's unfettered creativity. In notes for his autobiography, Prince highlighted the liberatory power of such creativity, writing that he wanted his book to be about "the freedom to create autonomously. Without anyone telling you what to do or how or why.... I want to tell people to create. Just start by creating your day. Then create your life." Highlighting his strong association between purple and artistic creation, Prince sings in "Purple Music" (an outtake from *1999* included on the Super Deluxe edition), "Ain't got no theory, ain't got no rules. / I just let the purple music tell my body what to do."

Prince's and Dove's affinity for Harold suggests reasons why artists are drawn to the book, but racial similarity does not predict reader identification. Ware, a white cartoonist, saw "Harold's tinted skin…as much a shell to be inhabited by the reader as Harold himself inhabited his purple creations." That said, I've always wondered whether the darker-skinned Harold on the cover of the Chinese edition of *Harold and the Purple Crayon* (C8) was an attempt to increase the book's appeal to local readers—even though Harold remains the same "10% brown" color within the pages of the book itself.

25

Translating Harold

In translation, Harold is not always Harold, his crayon is not always a crayon, and its color is not always purple. In Chinese, Harold is 阿罗 ("Aluo"). The current Swedish edition calls him Harald, but two previous versions name him Pelle—the diminutive of the names Per, Pär, and Peter. In Danish, he is Tullemand (C9). This is not a proper name, but rather a term of endearment for a little boy. In Dutch, he is Paultje—a diminutive of Paul that might translate to Pauley in English. Where Swedish, Danish, and Dutch children see a name marked by an adult's tendency to infantilize, young Fins meet a child with a name used by adults. In Finnish, Harold is Valtteri, a version of the name Walter.

These differences are neither flaws nor the result of a careless translator. As Walter Benjamin reminds us, "No translation would be possible if in its ultimate essence it strove for likeness to the original." Instead, "The task of the translator consists in finding that intended effect [*Intention*] upon the language into which he is translating which produces in it the echo of the original." Translations are not intentional distortions. They are interpretations that grant a work an afterlife in a different language—in this case, highlighting different facets of Harold's story. In the first German translation, the title *Ich mach mir meine eigne Welt* emphasizes the world-making power of Harold's crayon (C10). (In English, that title is *I make my own world*.) In the current German translation, *Harold und die Zauberkriede*, the purple crayon becomes *magic chalk* (C11). If more easily erased than crayon, chalk also has stronger associations with sidewalk art—children drawing in the world beyond the home. In this sense,

How to Draw the World: Harold and the Purple Crayon *and the Making of a Children's Classic.* Philip Nel, Oxford University Press. © Oxford University Press 2024. DOI: 10.1093/oso/9780197777596.003.0026

chalk gestures to the reality of Harold's adventure, as he explores and creates the world.

Other translations give Harold (or Aluo, Pelle, Paultje, Valtteri, Tullemand) a crayon, and they usually color it purple or violet. But in the 2001 French translation (C12), it is *rose* (pink). In the original German translation and in Swedish, it is red—*roten* and *röda*, respectively. The Chinese text calls it a colored crayon but leaves the color unspecified. Though Johnson identifies the color as purple, the crayon's pigment in the original *Harold* books is more ambiguous—and then different again in *A Picture for Harold's Room*. Because it is an "I Can Read Book," *Harold's Room* uses a darker purple than the other six *Harold* books. As HarperCollins's Senior Art Director Rick Farley explained to me, "I Can Read Books" generally uses a four-color printing process (black, cyan, magenta, yellow), but, for *Harold's Room*, Harper adds a fifth color for the crayon line—a purple ink that has been custom-mixed by the printer. For the other six *Harold* books, contemporary print runs use Pantone 247, the color of which could be described as light purple or a dark pink.

Given what he was facing when he invented Harold, Johnson might well have wryly chuckled at the *pink* and *red* translations. Maybe the feds weren't the only ones who suspected he was a radical?

26

Harold and the Red Crayon?

Though the book contains no reference to it, Johnson wrote the story while under investigation by the FBI. In the early 1950s, J. Edgar Hoover initially thought Johnson was a "concealed Communist," but by 1954 thought he might be a loyal enough citizen to become an informant. He authorized two New Haven FBI agents to approach Johnson about this possibility. Several times a week, for a couple of months, they sat in a car outside his home, watching him. He refused to come out and talk to them, and they ultimately gave up, four months before Harold's publication.

Was Johnson a Communist? Not in the 1950s. However, in the 1930s, he was certainly a communist with a lower-case c and might have been a Communist with an upper-case C: Johnson believed in international socialism, but it's unclear whether he was a member of the Communist Party. In the early 2000s, I searched microfilms of Communist Party USA records, but could not find any mention under David Johnson Leisk (Johnson's given name), Crockett Johnson (his better-known pseudonym), or Dave Johnson (friends called him "Dave"). He did have strong ties to the Left. From 1936 to 1940, he was art editor for *New Masses*, a radical weekly for which he was also a contributing cartoonist (from 1934 to 1940). In 2001, I spoke with A. B. Magil, who in 1938 joined *New Masses* as editor because Earl Browder—then General Secretary of the CPUSA—wanted to make sure the publication had "what the Party members considered firm political leadership." Since he worked alongside Johnson for two years *and* had joined the publication to make sure it hewed closely to the Party line, Magil was in an excellent position to confirm Johnson's

How to Draw the World: Harold and the Purple Crayon *and the Making of a Children's Classic.* Philip Nel, Oxford University Press. © Oxford University Press 2024. DOI: 10.1093/oso/9780197777596.003.0027

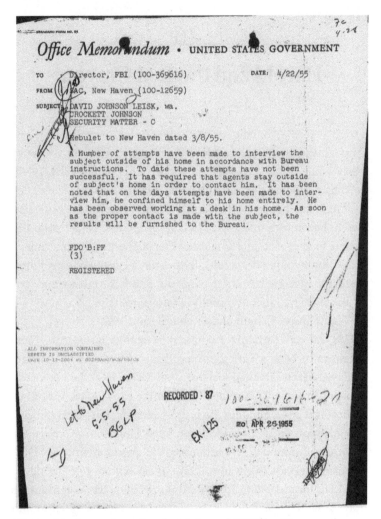

Figure 26. A page from Crockett Johnson's FBI file: Memorandum from FBI's New Haven Office to FBI Director J. Edgar Hoover, April 22, 1955. The 114-page file concludes the following month.

affiliations. Magil told me that he "always assumed that Dave was a Party member." He conceded, "I may be wrong about that," noting that Johnson "was a very quiet man" who "devoted his time to work and not to conversation." However, Magil added, "I think he was considered a Party member, as were most of the people who were working then on the magazine."

If Johnson ever was a Party member, I suspect he left in 1940, in the wake of the Molotov–Ribbentrop Pact (1939), a non-aggression treaty between the Soviet Union and Germany signed one week before the Nazis invaded Poland. The pact alienated many on the Left. I also know that Johnson actively supported FDR in 1944, contributing a cartoon to his re-election campaign. Johnson not only campaigned for Progressive Party presidential candidate Henry Wallace (FDR's Vice President during his third term) in 1948 but was also among the artists and intellectuals who met with Wallace in December 1947, encouraging him to run. Throughout his life, Johnson remained sympathetic to international socialism, but he was not a Party member when the FBI was watching him.

He did know that he was being watched. In August 1950, one FBI agent knocked on his front door. Johnson opened it and chatted, while a second agent covertly took his photograph. Johnson was named multiple times in two House Un-American Activities reports published in 1950 and 1951. By 1954, the US government was targeting people Johnson supported or knew personally, and it had succeeded in jailing several.

Given the conditions under which he wrote *Harold and the Purple Crayon*, it is tempting to read the book as an autobiographical fantasy in which Johnson (via his surrogate, Harold) escapes surveillance via the imagination: he is free in his mind, at least. Alternately, we might read the transformative power of Harold's imagination as political commentary, prefiguring 1960s French student radicals' slogan "All power to the imagination" and recalling Percy Bysshe Shelley's claim that the imagination was "the greatest instrument of moral good," and that poetry—a vital aid to imagination—heralded "the awakening of a great people to work a beneficial change in opinion or institution."

Though those interpretations are enticing, the book also offers a succinct expression of the powers *and* perils of the imagination. It is not an uncritical celebration of imaginative possibility: Harold nearly drowns and almost plummets to his death. Significantly, his fall from the mountaintop marks the longest time (three pages) that Harold's crayon leaves the page. Put another way: he comes closest to his demise when, mid-adventure, he relinquishes the symbol of his creative mind. He stops thinking. *Harold and the Purple Crayon* does highlight the many attractions of imaginative play, but it also warns us to be mindful of how we imagine. It isn't just saying *keep your wits and your purple crayon,* but rather *never use your purple crayon (or imagination) thoughtlessly.* Imagine, but keep thinking as you do.

27
Dream or Nightmare?

When the book concludes with Harold going to bed, he never leaves this imaginary realm. In contrast, Wendy and her brothers travel from Neverland back to the Darling nursery, Alice awakens from Wonderland back into the real-world picnic, and Max leaves the wild things to return home. But Harold remains in the existential uncertainty of the blank page. For Chris Ware, this is alarming: "The metaphysical implications of this hugely isolating ending still upset me. But presented with Johnson's characteristically gentle whimsy, the page-turning impetus that gets you there feels just timed enough with the momentum of thought that it all goes down more or less painlessly." Ware is not alone in this sentiment. When the *New York Times*'s Lisa Belkin invited readers to name "children's picture books you hate," Genevieve from Decatur, Georgia named *Harold and the Purple Crayon*, admitting "I avoided touching our family copy of it when I was a kid. It confirmed my 6 year old existentialist fear that there was no reality outside my own head. Making a totally strange place home by drawing a window framing the moon may be an adult metaphor, but it is awfully cold comfort for a child."

I don't find it upsetting, but it is a little ambiguous. On the one hand, Harold's ability to draw his room and (literally) make his bed suggests that we can create home wherever we are: the imagination will always provide us a furnished dwelling. On the other, a hand-drawn house on a flat page is the *only* home Harold has in this seven-book series. He's trapped in a Baudrillardian simulacra, and yet...he seems happy there.

How to Draw the World: Harold and the Purple Crayon *and the Making of a Children's Classic.* Philip Nel, Oxford University Press. © Oxford University Press 2024. DOI: 10.1093/oso/9780197777596.003.0028

Perhaps "it all goes down more or less painlessly" (as Ware says) because Johnson approaches these questions in the spirit of philosophical inquiry. As Claire Bartholome says, *Harold and the Purple Crayon* raises the questions: "Must things be experiential in order to be real? Or can they exist simply in our minds?" As she suggests, the book's ambiguous reality brings to mind "the debate of the empiricists versus the rationalists. Rationalists like Descartes tended to believe that the reality of objects was in our ability to rationally understand them." In contrast, "empiricists like Locke felt that the interaction with objects in a physical way gave them a sense of universal reality." In *Harold and the Purple Crayon*, Descartes and Locke debate each other, but Johnson is content to conclude the book without resolving the debate. Harold thinks, therefore he draws. But if Harold makes the world, that world also makes Harold.

The book begins and ends in paradoxes, invites us to dwell *in* these contradictions, but somehow not to dwell *on* them. Perhaps its compelling story and minimalist aesthetic re-directs readers' attentions back to their own creative challenges—those blank pages that each of us face, armed with only our wits, our imaginations, and our experiences. Blurring boundaries between art and life, the book has inspired readers of many backgrounds to be creative—whether as a professional cartoonist, poet, illustrator, novelist, or as an amateur, creating for the sheer joy of doing so. Finding home in nothingness, challenging readers to confront their blank canvases, *Harold and the Purple Crayon* invites us to dream and to think.

28

The End

Johnson's capacity for dreaming yielded more ideas than he had time to pursue. For six consecutive years (1955–1960), he produced a new *Harold* book, each of which ventured into a new genre: metafiction (which is true of all the *Harold* books), fairy tale, science fiction, Christmas story, circus story, reading primer. After the sixth of these, there would be no new *Harold* book or any other Crockett Johnson children's book for three more years.

One reason was the sheer number of other projects he was involved in. It's remarkable that Johnson managed to write six *Harold* books in so short a time. In 1958 and 1959, he was also doing advertising work for both Punch Films and Film Designers. In 1959 alone, he published four children's books, only one of which was about Harold. That same year, he was working on the pilot episode for a new *Barnaby* series, starring Bert Lahr (the Cowardly Lion in the *Wizard of Oz*) as Mr. O'Malley, and 5-year old Ronny Howard as Barnaby—a role that caught the eye of TV producer Sheldon Leonard, who, in casting him as Opie on *The Andy Griffith Show* (1960–1968), launched Howard's career. In early December, Johnson and Krauss flew to Hollywood to attend rehearsals and filming. Later that month, *Barnaby and Mr. O'Malley* aired on CBS to strong reviews.

Even a mind as inventive as Johnson's can only do so much at once.

There's some evidence of his divided attention in the 1960 book—*A Picture for Harold's Room*. In the original July 1959 dummy, Johnson has Harold walking back the way he came, which would mark the sole time he goes backwards in any of the

How to Draw the World: Harold and the Purple Crayon *and the Making of a Children's Classic.* Philip Nel, Oxford University Press. © Oxford University Press 2024. DOI: 10.1093/oso/9780197777596.003.0029

purple-crayon adventures. Perhaps struck by the oddity of this choice, Harper reader Ann Jorgensen suggested that instead of having "Harold go back across the mountains and the sea," Johnson might have Harold "draw himself in his room" to show "how Harold found he could return easily." Jorgensen pointed out that Harold is, at this point in the book, "worried about returning," and she was concerned that children would "worry with him." Johnson agreed, restoring Harold's—and the story's—forward momentum. In the finished book, he has Harold cross out the picture, step onto a blank page, and draw himself home.

Johnson may also have hesitated to write a seventh *Harold* book because he did not like to repeat himself. When the TV pilot renewed interest in *Barnaby*, he reluctantly returned to and then abandoned what was then his most famous creation. Working with Warren Sattler, he updated *Barnaby*'s plots for the 1960s, and the strip again appeared in newspapers. After a year and a half, he quit *Barnaby* for the final time. He had new ideas for children's books that interested him more than his old strip. Unfortunately, Harper was less interested in his newer, more philosophical work. It published only two of the six children's books he created after 1960.

But Ursula Nordstrom really wanted another Harold book. Johnson told her that he would create "another Harold book...if I had an idea or a subject." Might she ask managing editor Susan Hirschman "to write a jacket blurb in a spare moment"? If he had a blurb, Johnson said, "I am sure I will be able to write a book for it. A couple of times, as I've said, I have wished I had the blurb before I got tangled in the book."

Perhaps noting the philosophical turn in his recent work, Hirschman in April 1961 sent him a jacket flap copy for what she called *Harold's Republic*. It began like this:

> "Here is the flap copy," said Harold, "and anyone knows that books have flap copy. Therefore, if there is flap copy, it stands to reason that there must be a book."

And her flap copy concluded like this:

> Crockett Johnson's many fans, as well as all students of philoso-
> phy, will recognize the truth of the following syllogism:
>   Books are good.
>   When Crockett Johnson writes one, they're better.
>   This new book about Harold is Crockett Johnson's best.

From that germ of an idea grew *Harold's ABC*, the final and most innovative of Johnson's *Harold* books.

Increasing the challenge of writing an ABC book, Johnson made this one a continuous narrative that linked each letter to the next. If that weren't sufficiently difficult, each object also forms part of the object or idea it names. A creates the slanted roof of a house's Attic, B is two Books (viewed from the side) in a stack, K is part of a Kite, L makes a right angle in a zig-zagging streak of Lightning. Many letters begin more than one word. Visually, G forms the head of a Giant. Johnson's narrator then adds five more "G" words, telling us that "Giants generally aren't so genial. But this one grinned" and that he "gently set him on the ground." Some letters veer towards the abstract, as in I for Idea (the I forms the vertical line of an exclamation point) or N for Nobody (peaks of Mountains, extending the landscape of the "M" word, but emphasizing that no one else is there). Atypically, this book ends with Harold drawing himself out of sight. Behind the fence in his Yard, one solitary hand and its crayon are visible. On the book's final page, only Harold's artwork remains. From his bedroom window, seven increasingly larger Z's drift out toward us. The text concludes: "In his bedroom, as he dozed off, he made up a word. Z is for Zzzl, or little snore."

After 1965, Johnson abandoned children's books entirely, return-ing only to illustrate Ruth Krauss's *The Happy Egg* (1967). He would devote the rest of his life to mathematics and original paintings based on theorems. But he did come back to Harold one final time.

In early July 1975, just before lung cancer ended Johnson's life, his friend, the psychiatrist Gil Rose, sat at his bedside in Norwalk Hospital. Johnson was in pain, scared, and drifting in and out of consciousness. To help him manage his fear, Rose asked: "Well, what would Harold do?" Johnson thought about death from Harold's perspective, and he calmed down.

He died a few days later, at the age of 68.

29

Harold and Me

When Crockett Johnson died, I was six years old, living two and a half hour's drive north of him, in Lynnfield, Massachusetts. As an adult, I have sometimes wished that I had asked my parents to drive me down to visit the author of my favorite book. But I did not then know that Johnson lived in Connecticut. I did not know any authors. I did not know that you could seek them. If I had known, I doubt I would have. I was a shy child who loved to read, more at home in my imagination than out in the world.

I suspect that I was attracted by the book's vivid sense of how the imagination can change reality. It affirmed what stories did to me. Whether reading or writing them, stories both transported me to other worlds and changed the way I saw my own.

Yet despite my early affinity for it, the book is completely absent from my memories of early childhood. *Harold and the Purple Crayon* appears only in memories *of* those memories. When I was in eighth grade, my mother got a job teaching at a private school, enabling my sister and me to attend at no additional cost. During each month's faculty meeting (held after the end of the school day), my sister and I were left alone in the school library to do our homework. She did her homework. I did not. Instead, I wandered over to the picture books and rediscovered *Harold and the Purple Crayon*—which I then recognized as a childhood favorite. I pulled it from the shelf and began re-reading. Enveloped in Johnson's story, I felt myself temporarily transported back to early childhood. After I finished, I looked up and noticed on the shelf other books starring Harold—*Harold's Trip to the Sky* and *Harold's*

How to Draw the World: Harold and the Purple Crayon *and the Making of a Children's Classic.* Philip Nel, Oxford University Press. © Oxford University Press 2024. DOI: 10.1093/oso/9780197777596.003.0030

ABC. Had I read these when I was younger, too? I wasn't sure. I read them next and found them just as enchanting.

So, at the age of fourteen—an age when you might expect me to be reading young adult novels—I began to collect paperbacks of the *Harold* books. Each time I entered a bookstore in those pre-Internet days, I headed straight for the children's section and looked for these small books, gradually building a collection of six of the seven *Harold* titles. (*Harold at the North Pole* was out of print.)

I think that, as a shy teenager at a new school, I may have found comfort in the idea that creativity would help me find my way, and felt reassured that I could find my place in the world simply by imagining it. On a deeper level, getting reacquainted with Harold returned me to the delights of early childhood, such as: the magic of discovering, at age 3, that I could read; the thrill of getting pulled into a story; and what would become a lifelong fascination with language and art. The book reconnected me to a curiosity mostly quashed during my seven years of public school. My travels with *Harold and the Purple Crayon* when I was a teen (and since!) were never an escape into fantasy. They were and are a way of grounding myself in what matters most to me.

As I write these sentences, it occurs to me that perhaps my entire book is, in part, an attempt to understand why Johnson's book continues not only to speak to me, but to impart new ideas each time I re-read it. When, at the end of the next chapter, you finish reading this book, I will not have finished writing it. It is "finished" in the sense that it is edited, formatted, designed, bound (if you are reading a codex), and available for purchase or for checking out of a library. It remains incomplete because, though this may surprise you, I have more to say—some of which is already swirling around in my head, and some of which has not yet occurred to me. I stopped at thirty chapters merely because thirty is a nice round number, and I had to stop somewhere. But *Harold and the Purple Crayon* has not stopped animating my thoughts.

Children's books have much to teach those of us who are no longer children. There are levels of meaning we may have missed when we were younger. Adults may reach understandings unavailable to less experienced readers, just as children may arrive at interpretations lost to adults who have forgotten their own childhoods. In children's literature, there is art, insight, and beauty for readers of all ages.

30

Harold and You

What about you?

1. Why did *Harold and the Purple Crayon* capture your childhood imagination, if it did?
2. If *Harold* did not interest you when you were a child, why does it interest you now? (Why are you reading this book?)
3. If you read any of the *Harold* books as a child, did you identify with Harold? Why? Or why not?
4. If you felt an affinity for Harold, did any of your identity categories (race, gender, etc.) align with your understanding of Harold's identity categories? Did these alignments make Harold seem more "like you"?
5. Did you see Harold as masculine, feminine, both, or neither? Did you see him as white, Black, Brown, or aligned with a different racial or ethnic category?
6. Does the color of the crayon motivate the direction of the narrative? Within six weeks of its publication, *Harold and the Purple Crayon* was selling so well that Ursula Nordstrom was encouraging Johnson to write a sequel: "I know you don't want to do *Harold and His <u>Green</u> Crayon* or *Harold and His <u>Orange</u> Crayon*, but I honestly think further adventures of Harold would sell and not be a cheap idea, either." Johnson's sequels all keep the crayon purple. However, what if he had followed her suggestion? Would other colors—green, orange, blue—suggest other types of adventures? If Harold drew versions of the stories in Johnson's sequels, would different colors inspire different narrative choices, and what would those choices be?

How to Draw the World: Harold and the Purple Crayon *and the Making of a Children's Classic*. Philip Nel, Oxford University Press. © Oxford University Press 2024. DOI: 10.1093/oso/9780197777596.003.0031

7. What adventure should Harold pursue next? What would the full-page mural of that dream look like? At what key moments in the mural's creation would you pause to show Harold drawing? How does the path of the crayon suggest the ideas that lead to the next page of the story?

8. Johnson's stories invite us to watch Harold's creative work in progress. What other artistic forms include an audience witnessing the art taking shape? Architecture? Free jazz? Improvisational theatre? Something else? Which of these is most closely analogous to the *Harold* books? Why?

9. Why does Harold make art? If you create art (any kind, any medium), why do *you* make art?

10. If you do not yet make art, put this book down and go make some—any kind, in any medium. Sing a song or invent one. Compose a poem. Or draw a picture of what you see—something outside of the window, something you wish were outside of the window, or something inside of your head. What did you learn from your artistic experiment? What did making art help you see or understand?

11. What might be gained by looking at the world from Harold's perspective? Have you ever asked yourself, "What would Harold do?" If you have, what was the result?

12. Can art change the world?

13. If Harold is both creator of his world and created by his world, how much of his experience is within his control and how much is beyond his control?

14. Inasmuch as you both create and are created by your world, would any of Harold's strategies help shift the balance of power in your favor, even if ever so slightly?[1] If so, which one(s)?

15. In two of the *Harold* books, Harold crosses out what he has drawn. But he cannot erase his crayon line. Why give Harold a difficult-to-erase medium (like the crayon) instead of something easily erasable (like chalk or a pencil)? If Harold could

erase, how would these books change? What might be the ripple effects of the erasure?

16. As Chapter 27 notes, the idea of drawing your own world on a blank page has inspired some readers and frightened others. Is Harold's life a dream or a nightmare? Would you trade your life for his? Or, *under what conditions* would you trade your life for his?

17. If you had a world-making crayon like Harold's, what would you do with it?

18. What is your purple crayon? Or: What does Harold's crayon represent, *for you*?

19. At what age do children typically understand the mysterious logic of *Harold and the Purple Crayon*? If you remember reading *Harold* as a child, at what age did you begin to understand it? If any children in your life have read the book, at what age did they begin to understand it?[2]

20. If you read the *Harold* books as a child, how has your understanding of the books changed over time?

21. Which left a greater impact on your memory—*Harold and the Purple Crayon*'s words or its images? I ask for two reasons. First, Rita Dove remembers the book as wordless: Noting that she "must have been four or five" at the time of reading it, she writes that *Harold and the Purple Crayon* "has no words and its pictures are only in black and white." Second, the long history of iconoclasm indicates that many people consider images to be more powerful than words. As David Freedberg writes, the impulse to destroy images derives from the fear that images "are somehow *more* than art, that they are what they represent." So, for you, which creates a more durable impression—words or images?[3]

22. How should we distinguish between real and imaginary? Are ideas, dreams, or emotions as real as physical objects? How might the answers to these questions differ depending upon a person's age or other circumstances?

23. What is the missing chapter of this book? What other questions should we ask of *Harold and the Purple Crayon*?
24. What questions would you ask Harold?
25. What questions would you ask Crockett Johnson?
26. What questions would you like to ask me?
27. What book or artwork from your youth do you find yourself returning to? Why does this work continue to tug at your attention?
28. What book or other work fascinates *you* enough to sustain such deep, close reading? What in the work itself animates your imagination? And what in your relationship with the work calls you back to it?

You don't have to answer all or even any of these questions. But do take a moment to reflect. By way of encouragement, the next two pages are blank.

Jot down some ideas. Ask questions of your own.

Or just pick up your purple crayon, and start drawing.

Afterword

Harold in the World

I wish I could see your art (if you decided to draw or paint), read what you wrote (if you elected to write), or enjoy the combination of pictures and words (if you chose to create a picture book or comic strip).

So, if you feel moved to share, please send your words and images to ourpurplecrayons@gmail.com. Thank you!

Initially, at least, your submissions will be a one-way exchange. I'll see your ideas and images, but other readers of this book will not. In time and with labor, I could build an on-line gallery to gather your creative efforts, and then to share them more broadly. Or, if this book becomes successful enough to warrant a second edition, I could write a new chapter, including representative selections from your submissions.

But these possible futures are unknowable. And, in any case, we're in the afterword now: the book is now officially over!

Unless you're still reading it.

For you loyal few who have decided to continue on into this afterword, we're embarking on a guided tour through *Harold* in the popular imagination. As we explore the impact of the *Harold* books, I'll be offering answers to some of the questions raised in the previous chapter. From the moment *Harold and the Purple Crayon* landed in the world, its influence began rippling outwards. This is a map of those ripples.

How to Draw the World: Harold and the Purple Crayon *and the Making of a Children's Classic.* Philip Nel, Oxford University Press. © Oxford University Press 2024. DOI: 10.1093/oso/9780197777596.003.0032

Which, sure, are challenging to map.

So, like all maps, this one is necessarily selective. As cartographer Mark Monmonier says, any map is "but one of an indefinitely large number of maps that might be produced from the same data." Though this afterword is longer than any of the preceding thirty chapters (and you would certainly be forgiven if you chose to skip it!), we will not visit every adaptation of *Harold and the Purple Crayon*, nor catalogue every work that bears its influence. A useful map must always omit, whether it is helping you find your way to a picnic of nine pies, or charting Harold's journey through the minds of his readers. Good maps include only that which is essential to navigation, but what is "essential" depends very much on what you want to see and where you want to go. That is why, even after reading this afterword (or, better, *before* reading it), you should follow at least one of the suggestions in the previous chapter, and begin drawing your own maps.

Why attempt so subjective an endeavor as measuring a work's impact on its readers? Well, because we read them when we are at our most impressionable, beloved children's books can leave an outsized impression on our adult selves. They become part of our psyche because our absorbent child brains assimilate these stories in a deeper, more intimate way than our adult brains would. They become fixtures in our lives because we read these books when we are very much in the process of becoming, trying to make sense of the world and our place in it.

Tracing Harold's adventures in the world beyond the book—in various media, including adaptations—is also easier than it at first may seem. The specific *Harold* elements thematized in an influenced work offer clues to how Johnson's book lives in that person's imagination. And, since "faithful" adaptation is impossible, the differences between Johnson's original and any new version reveals what its adapters think is most important.

The Medium and the Message

In case anyone tripped over the phrase "'faithful' adaptation is impossible," consider that when a story migrates from one medium to another, it *needs* to be different. For a sixty-four-page picture book to become a play, a feature film, a TV series, an app, or political satire, the original work must change. As Linda Hutcheon points out, "technical constraints of different media will inevitably highlight different aspects of that story."

Given its technological potential, the app seems an ideal medium for a story about imaginative possibility. Via an immersive experience akin to that of a modern video game, an app might create a simulation in which users can "become" Harold. I could imagine Christoph Niemann developing an experience like his *Chomp* app, in which users insert video of their faces into animated scenes from *Harold*, or, better, get to draw their own story. Trilogy Studios' *Harold and the Purple Crayon* app, which briefly topped Apple's iPad Books App bestseller list in 2011, does invite us into a fantasy of leaving our world for one in which we can draw our own adventures. As *Common Sense Media*'s review of the app proclaimed, "kids are asked to 'be' Harold's crayon."

However, that claim is only somewhat true. The app allows you to "draw" Harold's line by swiping your fingers across the iPad, but—no matter how you swipe—the lines appear exactly as Harold drew them. Recreating exactly the same line each time is not a convincing illusion of "being" Harold's crayon. In any case, who wants to be a crayon? We want to be the artist. We want to be Harold. Though that is of course impossible, an app could make creative use of the strengths and limitations of the technology rather than insist that we just trace Harold's line through the story.

As a result, the difference between the 1955 picture book and the 2011 app is the difference between experiencing art and following a set of instructions. Via identifying with Johnson's iconic protagonist, readers of the book can both imagine themselves as artists and experience art that is apparently in the process of being created. In contrast, the app insists that you perform a rigid digital script. In having us replicate a pre-existing line, the app does not even allow us the freedom of a coloring book, where we can at least color outside of the lines.

The medium shapes the message but is not itself the message. The ideas in Johnson's book can be translated into different media, but not if the translator is trying to make a literal one-to-one "equivalent."

Metafiction

In contrast, *Harold*-inspired works by Chris Van Allsburg and Dav Pilkey ask: What would it mean to bring Crockett Johnson's metafictional themes into a different medium or genre? Directly addressing what he has called the "fairly elusive, mysterious idea" of his favorite childhood book, Chris Van Allsburg in *Bad Day at Riverbend* (1995) wonders what it is like to be not the crayon, but the paper. Through its conflict between the residents of Riverbend and the crayons of a young reader, the book asks "How would a character in a coloring book experience reality? What would that coloring-book character see?"

Told from the perspective of the characters in a *Cowboy Coloring Book*, Van Allsburg's *Bad Day at Riverbend* has cowboys rendered in black-outlined coloring-book style both confront and ultimately succumb to the crayons of a little girl—likely modeled on Van Allsburg's daughter Sophia, the "Little Buckaroo" to whom the book is dedicated. Readers of Van Allsburg's picture book recognize these energetic scribbles as the effects of a crayon, but the people of Riverbend are mystified by these "great stripes of some kind of shiny, greasy slime" covering horses, cattle, buildings, and some of the cowboys. At story's end, cowboys charge forward to face the danger, and get "frozen in the bright light that suddenly filled the sky"—which, Van Allsburg's art reveals, is the effect of the girl's crayon scribbling over them. On the picture book's final page, she has closed the book. So, for the characters, "the light went out." Though many of his children's books dramatize how dreams bend reality, *Bad Day at Riverbend* is Van Allsburg's most obvious homage to Harold, and a reminder that the fun of altering reality depends very much on who the artist is.

In Dav Pilkey's *Captain Underpants* books (1997–), fourth-graders Harold (named for Johnson's character) and George (named for Curious George) both enjoy and regret altering reality, which in turn invites metafictional meditations on storytelling itself. Drawn by Harold (of course!) and imagined by George, the homemade *Captain Underpants* comics—Pilkey's story-within-a-story—finds the titular hero, in the first book, battling "the inedible Hunk" (born of "stinky tacos" the students have thrown out) and "fighting for truth, justise [*sic*], And ALL that is Pre-shrunk and cottony." Just as *Harold's Fairy Tale* and *Harold's ABC* play with (respectively) the conventions of fairy tales and ABC books, Pilkey's characters are spoofing the generic features of superhero comics. And, echoing the *Harold* books' premise that we are witnessing Harold in the act of creating his story, *Captain Underpants* often references its own story-in-progress, as when, in the first book, George says to Harold, "You know, up until *now*, this story was almost *believable*." Each *Captain Underpants* book also includes a "Flip-o-rama" section in which Harold and George address its readers, asking us to flip back and forth between sets of two consecutive pages, the effect of which is to animate the action.

Though censorious adults often seek to ban the *Captain Underpants* books for "encouraging disruptive behavior" or being "unsuited to age group," Pilkey's Harold and George are neither purely reckless nor models of appropriateness. Where Johnson's narrative voice blurs any clear boundary between adult and child, Pilkey achieves a similar effect through his books' plots. On the one hand, we might say of Pilkey's characters what Maurice Sendak says of Johnson's protagonist: "Harold does exactly as he pleases. There are no adults to demonstrate or remonstrate." On the other, Pilkey's mischievous pair also must fulfill "adult" roles in restoring order: Harold and George both delight in misrule and take responsibility for what they have wrought. Pilkey's gross-out humor differs from Johnson's subtle wordplay, but both Harolds (and one George) expose the myth of an adult-child binary. And both the *Harold* books and the *Captain Underpants* books take children's imaginations seriously.

Taking Children Seriously

So, too, do the best adaptations of *Harold and the Purple Crayon*. In its word-for-word and scene-by-scene animated rendering of Johnson's book, David Piel's 7-minute 1959 cartoon meets this criterion. But I'm only going to write two more sentences about it. Though Piel's version is the very first time that *Harold and the Purple Crayon* migrates from one medium to another, its similarity to the original picture book makes it less interesting to contemplate than adaptations that make substantive changes to *Harold*. Also, you can watch Piel's version.

But you can't see the 1990 stage adaptation or read the mid-1990s movie script by Michael Tolkin, best known for writing the Oscar-nominated screenplay for *The Player* (1992). Tolkin's script (which I bought off eBay decades ago) was never produced. The play had a short run: after making its debut in New York's Promenade Theatre in November 1990, it toured through the early part of that decade. I never saw it, but I have read the script—courtesy of Theatreworks USA, the company that produced it.

I wish that we could see both of these. Each adaptation thoughtfully considers how to translate a two-dimensional medium (the picture book) into a three-dimensional one, and how to use the new medium to take seriously the inner lives of young people.

With music by Jon Ehrlich, lyrics by Ehrlich and Robin Pogrebin, and a book by Jane Shepherd, the first stage adaptation of *Harold and the Purple Crayon*—which its creators first performed in Ruth Krauss's living room in 1989—animates the elusive idea of Harold's reality-bending crayon by making its line alive.[1] Literally. Four Purple People, each clad in purple long johns and a purple hat, portray the drawing—and that's *drawing* as both act (verb) and effect (noun). As Shepherd says of the Purple People, they are "the agents of his imagination, executing the crayon's designs and moving the action forward." At some moments in the play, "they *become* the drawing, embodying an Apple Tree, the Dragon or the Moon, and other times they *are* the action, spinning Harold through the air when he falls off a mountain, and still other times they *set* the action up, presenting props in the places you least expect them." Having four of the show's five actors (all of whom are adults) portray the crayon's effects emphasizes how consequential Harold's imagination is.[2] As Ehrlich said of their adaptation (and Johnson's book), "It really was the story of creation. And it was packed with all kinds of lessons about creation and the responsibility...that comes with putting something out into the world."

While the 1990 musical follows the plot of the first *Harold* book, Michael Tolkin's unproduced script (1995) emphasizes the reality of Harold's imagination by showing the crayon's effects on two parallel narratives. Gesturing to the plot of *Harold's Trip to the Sky*, Tolkin creates a nine-month mission to Mars, led by Flight Commander Alison Kramer and introduced into Harold's world via a TV news report. The other narrative, also Tolkin's invention, is Harold's mother's pregnancy and its complications. Throughout the screenplay, when adults fail to take Harold's imagination seriously or insist on controlling it, negative effects ripple outward into the two other stories. When unfettered,

Figure 27. Cast of *Harold and the Purple Crayon*, clockwise from bottom left: Robert Tate, Robert Roznowski, Erin Hill, James Barbour, and Pauline Frommer. c. 1990. Reproduced courtesy of Theatreworks USA.

Harold's imagination increases his understanding, and allows him to help others. Early in Tolkin's script, in response to rain preventing the rocket from blasting off (which Harold and his parents are watching on television), Harold draws an umbrella over the rocket ship on a photograph in that morning's paper. Then, on TV, the rain at the launch site stops. His father yanks the newspaper away, leaving "an angry purple streak across the picture." On television, lightning flashes in the sky above the rocket. Harold grabs the newspaper back and draws a sun. On TV, sunshine returns, and the countdown to liftoff resumes. At the story's climax, when both parallel narratives appear to be headed for tragic ends, Harold and his crayon rescue the Mars mission, his sibling-to-be, and his mother. The journey is never without risk, but Harold's imagination saves the day.

To a greater degree than any other adaptation of, or work, influenced by *Harold*, Tolkin's script is acutely sensitive to the reality of children's interior lives. It understands that, for young people, imaginative play is not merely fanciful, but is how they learn to navigate a complicated world. I admire Tolkin's attention to the reality of young people's imaginations not only because it echoes Johnson's book, but because the inner lives of children shape the adults they become. As James Baldwin observed, "the interior life is a real life, and the intangible dreams of people have a tangible effect on the world."

Harold Grows Up

Addressing this subject directly, several recent works ask: What if Harold grew up? How would his imagination serve him then? As AJR, the pop trio composing music for a proposed 2024 *Harold and the Purple Crayon* Broadway show, put it, "We adored 'Harold and The Purple Crayon' growing up, and we thought: 'What if we saw Harold as a young adult, realizing that his problems are too profound to simply draw away?'" Dramatizing one answer to this question, a 2020 *New Yorker* cartoon by Suerynn Lee shows a grown-up Harold, a purple crayon in hand and a document on the desk in front of him (C13). He looks across the desk at a woman seated on the other side. She says, "Harold, I'm really going to need you to sign the divorce papers in blue or black ink."

D. Gilson's "Harold & the Purple Crayon" (2017), one of a series of poems imagining children's-book characters outside of the books, delivers the most fully developed exploration of an older Harold. Envisioning a college-age Harold talking with a psychologist, Gilson plays with the popular notion of art reflecting the artist's childhood trauma. The poem begins, "Berkeley psychologists told Harold / his anger was justified. What parents / let their child go for a midnight walk / under no moon?" After comically recasting Harold's unsupervised nighttime adventures as forms of parental neglect, the poem then wonders how a child genius copes with young adulthood: "Everyone knew Harold could draw. / By sophomore year, he was critiquing / grad students. By twenty, Harold knew / exactly when to quote Sontag." In the poem, Harold is so bright that his professors praise him but do not understand him. In response, his work becomes "increasingly angry: / apple trees, their fruit rotting in monochrome / purple, under the notable lack of a moon." It's a wryly funny poem, but also sympathetic to a misunderstood, alienated young adult.

Since Harold is played by adult actor Zachary Levi, I initially thought that the new live-action film might also offer a portrait of the artist as a young man. However, to extrapolate from the trailer, this Harold seems to be a mental child in the body of an adult human. Directed by Carlos Saldanha with a screenplay by David Guion and Michael Handelman, the movie will be released in August 2024—three months before this book will be published. So, if my prediction is incorrect, I invite you to take your purple crayon and cross out this paragraph.

Imagination as Narcissism

In 2018 and 2019, a more troubling version of an "adult" Harold arrived. Many people noticed that, if you subtract Harold's thoughtfulness and altruism, then imagination can easily become narcissism. As the first person to make this connection told me, "I looked at Harold closely, and was thinking about how he makes the world as he sees it, and makes it up as he goes. Which is what Trump does, and it just seemed to click." The result was *Donald and the Golden Crayon* (2018), the first book-length satire based on *Harold and the Purple Crayon* (C14). Though written by a prolific author of children's books, he published this book under the pseudonym "P. Shauers." As he explained, "I didn't want any librarians to think this was for kids, and I didn't want any right-wing nutjobs to go after my books in any way."

Combining the tone and sentence structure of the *Harold* books with the malevolence and pettiness of America's forty-fifth president, the book uses the crayon as a visual metaphor for Donald Trump's gaslighting. With a keen understanding of the tension between image and text, "Shauers" has Donald using the golden crayon to draw the very things that, he insists, do not exist. On one two-page spread, Donald draws a family huddled on the rooftop of their house, as rain falls, floodwaters rise, and Donald sails by in his golden boat (also drawn by the crayon). Referencing "houses that were underwater," the text says, "People who did not vote for Donald said it was climate change. Wrong! Climate change is a hoax created by the Chi-neese." Donald also draws what he *does* want to see—a brick wall, MAGA supporters, and a military parade. Near the book's end, Donald has a tantrum, throws his golden crayon at the TV, and the crayon breaks in half. He Tweets his disappointment: "What loser invented crayons? Too weak. They break too easily. So sad." He goes to sleep, dreaming of "Covfefe."

In early September of the following year, satire edged closer to reality when Mr. Trump wielded his sharpie in an attempt to alter the weather. Insisting that, contrary to the National Weather Service's predictions, Alabama "will most likely be hit much harder than anticipated," Mr. Trump used a black sharpie on a weather map to show Hurricane Dorian headed for Alabama. (This was days *after* Dorian had already veered away from Alabama and up the Atlantic coast.) Within days of Trump's altered map (and often on the same day), many more people made the connection between Donald and Harold. Working independently of one another, cartoonists and journalists created three different satires called "Donald and the Black Sharpie": *Columbia Missourian* cartoonist John Darkow (on September 6), *Washington Post* cartoonist Tom Toles (in collaboration with Dana Milbank, also on September 6), and CNN's Jake Tapper (on September 8). Jimmy Kimmel read "Donald and the Magic Sharpie" on his late-night TV show (on September 6), and Ward Sutton created an eight-panel cartoon titled "Donald and the Purple Sharpie" (published on September 15). In each, Donald uses his sharpie to create his own reality, drawing crowds of fans, a border wall, or a US flag on Greenland. That so many creative people would arrive at similar ideas so quickly suggests how deeply ingrained Harold and his crayon have become in the American imagination.

I suspect that the Donald-Harold comparison emerged not only because of their rhyming first names and investment in creating their own realities but because the joke works. Embodying Mr. Trump's childish petulance in a famous child emphasizes that behavior which might be forgivable and even funny from fictional children is neither when exhibited by an adult leader.

Inconsequential Imagination

Protecting a child from the consequences of his actions creates an adult narcissist and, in adaptations, it also removes the stakes that

Figure 28. John Darkow, *Donald and the Black Sharpie* (September 6, 2019). Courtesy of Cagle Cartoons, Inc.

make Johnson's original story exciting. Narrated by Sharon Stone, the thirteen-episode animated *Harold and the Purple Crayon* series (HBO, 2001–2002) sees imagination as a mostly benevolent creative force. Harold draws his world, and his world creates itself, objects coloring themselves in. In the pilot episode, he draws a river, which then turns itself blue and begins to flow. The porcupine and moose are immediately sentient and accompany him on his journey. Extending Harold's generosity to the world, later in that first episode (which borrows many plot elements from the first *Harold* book), the initially frightening dragon returns as a friend, bringing a bucket of now ripe apples to Harold, moose, and porcupine. I suspect that, imagining the youngest viewers as its intended audience, the series creators decided to emphasize calm and safety, and to reduce the possibilities for harm. The series won praise, one reviewer citing its "*Mister Rogers*-style calmness" and another calling it "good TV."

However, in diminishing the imagination's potential hazards, the HBO series also removes the tension that gets us emotionally involved in Harold's adventure. In each of Johnson's books, it's not immediately clear whether Harold's artistic choices will help or hinder him. The suspense in not knowing how each picture-in-progress will resolve also taps into the realities of children's imaginations, where there's a real urgency to creativity, as young minds learn to solve the problems they face or accidentally create.

Improvisation and Creativity

As the means for expressing Harold's creativity, the purple crayon has in the popular imagination come to represent imagination itself. The improvisational theatre group The Purple Crayon—founded by Yale students Eric Berg and Ian Jacobs in 1985—takes its name from Johnson's book. Its long-form improv is called The Harold. For group members, the name is an allusion to *Harold and the Purple Crayon*, but the origin of The Harold dates to the San Francisco improv group The Committee, where it was also an allusion, but not to Johnson's character. In about 1965, when the group was trying to decide what to call its improvised performances, group member W. A. Mathieu called out "Harold"—a joking reference to the scene in *A Hard Day's Night* (1964), when a reporter asks George Harrison what he calls his haircut, and George answers "Arthur." The Harold traveled to Chicago with improv legend Del Close, who refined it and taught it to Eric Berg, who in turn brought it to Yale's Purple Crayon.

In the 1990s, Harold's purple crayon also inspired Professor Amy S. Bruckman (at the time, still a graduate student) to use "purple-crayon.media.mit.edu" as the domain name for her pioneering MIT *MediaMOO*—a MUD (Multi-User Domain)

Object-Oriented virtual reality system. As she says, "the ethos [of Johnson's book] fit with the creative world for kids I was designing." That creative world was *MOOSE Crossing* (1996–2007), a text-based, on-line, self-directed learning environment in which children aged 8 to 13 learned to program and to practice writing creatively. Though young people playing and learning via technology is common today, this sort of interactive collaboration was then new.

A more engaging adaptation than the iPad's app, the analog game—manufactured by Briarpatch and created by Peter Kingsley and Rachel Ammon (1999)—also invites players to use their imaginations. It contains a stack of fifty-four cards featuring titled drawings (all in purple on white, about half representing items from the *Harold* books), along with a whiteboard and an erasable purple marker. Players turn over one card at a time, draw the object on the whiteboard, and use the word in a story. Each subsequent player adds to the story, either by using the already supplied narrative or by inventing a new one. A player can alter the specifics of the narrative but not the order of the cards—and that's the challenge. When players make a mistake (by not remembering the order), they are out, and become a monitor for those who are still in the game. Memory keeps the score, and creativity keeps you playing.[3]

Influence or Coincidence?

Harold and the Purple Crayon's suggestion that, as Van Allsburg says of his childhood experience of reading the book, "I could be in control and create my own world" shows up in all works bearing *Harold*'s influence. In Thacher Hurd's *Art Dog*, Arthur Dog—an art museum guard—can, in his guise as Art Dog, alter the world via his art. Accused of stealing the *Mona Woofa*, Art Dog paints a ladder up to the bars of his jail cell, climbs the ladder, paints the bars away, and sets out to catch the real thief. As Hurd told me in an email, "I've often thought that Harold would get along very well with Art Dog," and he acknowledged, "I did put in a subtle aside to *Harold and the Purple Crayon* in *Art Dog*. I love that book, and loved it as a kid."

Thacher Hurd, Rita Dove, Richard Powers, cartoonist Peter Kuper, picture-book creator Deborah Freedman, and director Spike Jonze, among others, have all acknowledged the influence of *Harold and the Purple Crayon*. But when a creative person does not announce their affection for Johnson's book, how can we spot an influence? I mean, maybe the person just likes crayons, drawing, or the color purple? Perhaps the similarities are mere coincidence?

For instance, in the first of what seems like countless allusions to *Harold and the Purple Crayon*, the copyright page of Aaron Becker's *Journey* (2013) has a boy holding a purple crayon—purple making it the one item on the page not a shade of brown or grey. On the page opposite, a girl is seated on the steps with her red scooter—it, too, the sole splash of color on the page. Shifting its attention to her, a subsequent page finds her in a grey-brown bedroom looking at a red crayon on the floor. On the adjacent page, her wall has become a blank canvas. She draws a doorway on it, and steps through into a three-dimensional world of color. As Harold does, she draws a boat, hot air balloon, and flying carpet—traveling on each. (The flying carpet is in *Harold's Fairy Tale*.) By the story's end, she meets the purple-crayon-carrying boy, and the two set off on an adventure that continues in *Quest* (2014) and *Return* (2016). Many reviewers noted the similarities between Becker's books and the *Harold* books.

Yet, when writer James Preller mentioned *Journey*'s "obvious... debt to Crockett Johnson's *Harold and the Purple Crayon*" and asked Becker whether the *Harold* books were important to him as a child, Becker responded: "Actually, I was never a big fan of that book! I think the drawings bugged me somehow." After he published *Journey*, people pointed out the similarities, and so Becker returned to *Harold and the Purple Crayon*. He admitted: "I was amazed at the similarities in the story! I probably would never have made *Journey* if I was aware that there was something so similar already out there!" While both books do emerge from the shared premise that children's imaginations can shape the world, I don't think their similarities are mere coincidence. Given the sheer number of commonalities and Becker's acknowledgment of reading *Harold* in childhood, I feel comfortable in claiming that *Harold and the Purple Crayon* was an unconscious influence on Becker's *Journey* and its sequels.

But commonality is not causality. For example, Simon of British cartoonist Edward McLachlan's *Simon in the Land of Chalk Drawings* (1969) and its three sequels (1971–1973) has, in the US, sometimes been mistaken for Harold—in part, I think, due to the popularity of a series of 5-minute animated shorts based on the *Simon* books (1974–1976). They aired on ITV in Britain and on CBS's *Captain Kangaroo* in the US, with the Captain (Bob Keeshan) as the narrator in the American version. Suggesting an allusion to Crockett Johnson's work, the cover of the first *Simon* book is purple, and McLachlan's name is in the same pinkish purple as Harold's crayon. The books also share some common plot elements. Both characters not only create real items but draw some of the same things, such as train tracks—Simon in his first book, and Harold in his sixth. Both draw and ride rockets in their third books: *Harold's Trip to the Sky* (1957) and *Simon and the Moon Rocket* (1972). These parallels are suggestive.

But they also may be more likeness than influence. Though *Harold* was first published in the UK in 1957, it's possible that Norwegian writer Zinken Hopp's *Trollkrittet* (1948)—first published in English as *The Magic Chalk* (1959)—inspired McLachlan's *Simon* books, since the protagonists of both use chalk to create real people, real animals, and real things.[4] Also, McLachlan's didactic emphasis differs from Johnson's subtle narration. While both characters must address the consequences of their actions, those consequences are a much stronger focus for Simon than they are for Harold. The central lesson of *Simon in the Land of Chalk Drawings* is teaching Simon to finish what he started. A chalk-drawn character calls attention to the many problems that Simon's unfinished drawings have inflicted on the inhabitants of the Land of Chalk Drawings. The train driver has a train, but no tracks. A dog lacks a tail to wag, birds lack wings, an elephant lacks ears, and partially drawn children lie in hospital beds— unable to play "because you left them unfinished," Simon's chalk guide admonishes him. So, Simon spends the entire book finishing his drawings.

As *Harold* has risen in prominence, the likelihood of coincidental common features decreases. However, in 1969, it was possible that a British cartoonist would be unfamiliar with this American children's book: though then available in Britain, Johnson's books have never been as popular in the UK as they are in the US. It's plausible that Simon has been mistaken for Harold in the US simply because Crockett Johnson's character is better known here.

Fifty years after Simon, even smaller similarities—such as the prominence of a purple crayon—feel as if they are at least allusions to Johnson's book. I want to argue that Aaron Reynolds and Peter Brown's *Creepy Crayon!* (2022)—the third in their *Creepy* picture book series—is *Harold and the Purple Crayon* as told by Poe or Goethe. The flip side of the HBO version's benevolent creativity, *Creepy Crayon!* also has a purple crayon embodying an imagination that can create without guidance from the artist. But in this story, the crayon is demonic. When Jasper Rabbit finds a purple crayon, he's at first delighted. It correctly spells all the words on his spelling test and aces his math test for him. Then, on a day he does not use it, the crayon writes "DON'T IGNORE ME." By this point, Jasper has become uncomfortable about receiving credit he didn't earn. But each time he attempts to get rid of it, the crayon keeps finding its way back. He tries locking it in a basement box and throwing its microwaved remains into the trash, but—like a possessed doll in a horror film—it keeps returning and winning new accolades that Jasper no longer wants. In its review, the *Horn Book* said that *Creepy Crayon!* is "*Harold and the Purple Crayon* meets *Faust*." But perhaps, like me, reviewer Shoshanah Flax tends to see all contemporary purple crayons as descendants of Harold. As curator Sarah Urist Green has observed, "When people write reviews, they are really writing a kind of memoir": Flax and I may be telling you more about ourselves than about Jasper and his creepy crayon or Harold and his purple one.

Any attempt to trace lines of influence will be at least somewhat speculative. UK artist Anthony Browne's *Bear Hunt* (1979), in which a white bear outwits two hunters via his reality-altering pencil, seems a descendant of *Harold*, though it could as easily be inspired by *Simon in the Land of Chalk Drawings*. Likewise, Allan Ahlberg and Bruce Ingman's *The Pencil* (2011)—in which a pencil draws a boy, and then much more, and then a paintbrush to help him—might also be a descendant of *Harold*, of *Simon*, of both, or of neither.

Scholars and other obsessive readers seek resonances, echoes of the work in the world. These resonances can be meaningful whether or not they are intentional.

Icon of Imagination

In mapping some of these resonances, this afterword suggests how Harold and his purple crayon have become a kind of cultural shorthand, a flexible metaphor for understanding big questions about childhood, creativity, politics, psychology, art, and the nature of reality. I'm aware that there are other, equally compelling ways to draw such a map. J. M. Barrie writes that it is hard to "draw a map of a child's mind, which is not only confused, but keeps going round all the time." I would add that it is harder still to trace the influence of childhood dreams on adult selves—especially because so many adults have forgotten their childhoods. But forgotten maps deserve our closest attention. They show us what we have learned unconsciously. They display "the territory of the dream-world created in fantasy," as Ebony Elizabeth Thomas says. And, like the cartography of Barrie's Neverland, the fantastic maps of children's minds can also include damaging ideas about who does and does not belong in stories—ideas absorbed without children's awareness or consent. As Thomas puts it, "Neverland can be problematic when not all children, youth, and young adults can land on its shore."

Fortunately, Harold's racial ambiguity and absence of strongly gendered traits has invited a diverse array of artists into his Neverland. That's why he's an early muse of Prince, Scott McCloud, Bryan Collier, Dav Pilkey, Ole Könnecke, and so many others.

An iconic character and an ambassador from childhood, Harold is a signpost to youthful confidence in imagination's power, the surety that dreaming can alter reality, and the freedom of a creativity without limits or doubts. This is why a May 2010 episode of *The Simpsons* featured Harold drawing the concluding "couch scene" of the opening credits. (After Harold draws the family on the couch, Homer says "Draw me some beer." Harold does.) It's why, in May 2014, designer Madeleine Stuart created a Harold display for Compas's store window in Los Angeles. As she said at the time, the book "illustrates that we all possess the ability to imagine, and then create, the world in which we live." With the moon framed in the window above his head, Stuart had a two-dimensional Harold finishing a drawing of his three-dimensional bed. Below him, in a Garamond typeface, she included an abridged quotation from near the book's end: "And then Harold made his bed...and drew up the covers." Also evoking the coziness of childhood bedtime, Jerry Scott and Jim Borgman devote seven panels of a 2009 Sunday *Zits* comic to *Harold and the Purple*

Crayon (C15). Though the strip's teenage protagonist Jeremy Duncan usually does not want to hang out with his parents, here he cheerfully recalls the book's plot with his mother until, in the final panel, he is fully absorbed in Harold's story and has again become a child ready for story time. Mrs. Duncan holds the book in her hands, Jeremy's gangly adolescent body curls up in her lap, and he says, "Start from the beginning."

That final panel gestures to why artists and thinkers are drawn to Harold. The book takes them back to the unselfconsciously creative, richly imaginative time of early childhood, when the boundary between fantasy and reality is paper-thin, when dreams can become real, and all you need to realize them is your imagination, scrap paper, and a crayon.

Notes

Chapter 12

1. Except during an eclipse, of course.

Chapter 13

1. For readers who enjoy notes about crayons: Between 1903 and 1914 (the year Johnson turned 8), a crayon labeled *violet* or *purple* refers to the same color. In 1914, the name *purple* (but not the color) vanished, returning in 1926 in several different varieties (all of which are distinct from violet).

Chapter 16

1. As I point out in my (currently unpublished) essay on the Howard strips, Johnson satirically invokes an "Indian" stereotype in order to refute it—but that refutation is not completely successful. Because stereotypes must be invoked to be satirized, attempts at satirizing always risk repeating the harm of the original caricature. The main focus of Johnson's satire is the savage/civilized binary that, as Philip Deloria's *Playing Indian* (1999) documents, is the central tension in white Americans' representations of Native Americans—embodied in the figure of the noble savage who is either a conveniently vanishing critique of Western society or a "savage" who must be destroyed to "protect" white invaders a.k.a. "settlers" (pp. 4, 5). When Howard speaks, he typically begins in the then-new stereotype of "Hollywood Indian-speak," then abruptly switches to fluent English, using a more elevated diction than the other characters—as if he feels obliged to give a performance of expected "Indian" speech before reverting to his natural eloquence. Johnson is mocking the notion that actual Native Americans speak as they're represented in popular culture, but the satire doesn't entirely work because, in its reliance upon a contrast between "savage" and "civilized," it reifies the binary opposition that it aspires to challenge. And that's a problem for much of *Barnaby*'s satire. It does not endorse these caricatures of "Indian-ness," but without knowledge of the stereotypes, the satire doesn't land as forcefully. It creates what Deloria in *Indians in Unexpected Places* (2004) calls the "ideological chuckle," in which viewers see this code-switching as merely a funny anomaly.

Chapter 24

1. Given Prince's capacity for self-invention, you'd be justified in wondering whether this claim is purely anecdotal. But it does appear to be accurate. Of Mattie Shaw (Prince's mother), Karlen says: "I had to take care when checking facts with Mattie: She'd agree with whatever Prince said was the truth .... Because I couldn't put a notion in her head or else she'd agree with whatever I said to be polite and agreeable, I had to wait almost a dozen years for her to volunteer without prompting, that Prince had indeed adopted purple as his favorite color in honor of his favorite children's book, *Harold and the Purple Crayon*" (pp. 30–31). Prince had told him this, but, Karlen says, "Baloney, I thought, when Prince told me the

story; it was the kind of piffle he'd peddled to credulous reporters all his life" (p. 31). Since he couldn't ask Shaw directly, he "asked her if Prince had liked to play pretend as a child." Shaw then relates the story I've included in the main text.

Chapter 30

1. Or, as Alexis Pauline Gumbs asks, "What are the boundaries we choose and do not choose?" (p. 87).
2. Maureen Crago and Hugh Crago's *Prelude to Literacy: A Preschool Child's Encounter with Picture and Story* (1983) offers one answer via its meticulous tracking of the Cragos' daughter Anna's response to various picture books, including *Harold*. In her third year, Anna begins trying to make sense of Johnson's book. At 3 years and 3 months, she is asking, "How can he make a balloon, and a basket, and people in it?" and "What can he draw them on?" (p. 206). By 3 years and 7 months, she wants to try Harold's ideas in the real world, asking her father, "How can I get up in the sky so I can draw on it with my purple crayon?" (p. 206). At 3 years and 9 months, she tests her hypothesis, using a pencil to draw on her home's brick wall "a house and swirls of smoke coming from the chimney." As the Cragos write, Anna is "coming to grips with the notion of an efficacious but inexplicable magic, a process that can have multiple, predictable effects, and which strongly contravenes the laws of nature as she knows them" (p. 207).

   If you're a researcher, how might you draw upon Anna Crago's experience to design a study tracking preschool children's responses to *Harold and the Purple Crayon*? What would you listen for in children's language or look for in their pictures? What questions (if any) would you ask of them?
3. I am pitting images against words to create a sharp question, but you'd be quite right in noting that "image vs. text" is something of a false dichotomy. Language can be figurative, creating images in your mind—as in "The sky was just a purple bruise" (from Elvis Costello's "Deep Dark Truthful Mirror") or "When the deep purple falls over sleepy garden walls / And stars begin to twinkle in the night" (from Mitchell Parish's lyrics to the Peter DeRose song "Deep Purple"). So, here are a couple of alternate questions. Which end of the image-text continuum creates a more durable impression in your mind? Are the pictures created by images more vivid than those created by words?

Afterword

1. Crockett Johnson's widow, Ruth Krauss, saw a version of the show in the spring of 1989 when its creators, seeking her permission, gave an ad hoc performance in her living room. Just six months later, in the fall of 1989, Krauss got a phone call from two screenwriters—Richard Gelb and Peter Brown of Meledandri/Gordon—pitching *Harold and the Purple Crayon* as a feature film.
2. The fifth actor—Robert Tate in the original production—portrays Harold.
3. Unlike the iPad app, this game still can be played—it's no longer in production, but used copies are available. (When the iPad received a system update in 2013, the *Harold* app stopped functioning, and subsequently disappeared from the app store.)
4. In this, the final note of the book, here's another instance of what is likely a shared influence. Though Jon Agee's *The Incredible Painting of Felix Clousseau* (1988) shares both the more conversational tone of Johnson's narrator and a protagonist whose art becomes real, the paintings of René Magritte are a stronger visual influence on Agee's book. One of Agee's two-page spreads seems to borrow the cannon from Magritte's *On the Threshold of Liberty* (1929). In this sense, both Agee and Johnson (who references Magritte on the title page of *A Picture for Harold's Room*) share a common ancestor.

Acknowledgments

I presented the first version of some of these chapters at the University of Winnipeg in June 2013. Between then and now, amid many other projects and commitments, I have kept returning to it, presenting different versions in invited talks, and it has gradually grown into this book. I hope the following paragraph acknowledges all who have assisted or encouraged me over the years, and yet I am quite sure that I have omitted many.

With apologies for all omissions, sincere thanks to Jen Aggleton, Misty Anderson, Stephen Barbara, Molly Bernstein, Ada Bieber, Johannes Binotto, Melanie Ramdarshan Bold, Amy Bruckman, Veronica Brusilovski, Kate Capshaw, Megan Montague Cash, Nina Christensen, Jackie Curtis, Gene Deitch, Jordan Dombrowski, Hannah Doyle, Sara Duke, Stewart Edelstein, Jon Ehrlich, Kristin Eshelman, Rick Farley, Else Frank, Harold Frank, Deborah Freedman, Tzofit Goldfarb, Terri Goldich, Naomi Hamer, Thomas Hamilton, Gloria Hardman, Susan Hirschman, Thacher Hurd, John Hyslop, Dee Jones, Vanessa Joosen, Paul Karasik, Sara Kearns, Gil and Kim Kernan, Catherine Keyser, Peggy Kidwell, Ole Könnecke, Peter Kuper, Jessica Lim, Christine Lötscher, A. B. Magil, Leonard Marcus, Marianne Martens, Michelle Martin, Jeanne McLellan, Bob and Helen McNell, Julia Mickenberg, Natasha Muhametzyanova, Mark Newgarden, Maria Nikolajeva, Susan B. Obel, Mervi Pakaste, Katie Rickard, Mavis Reimer, Mike Rex, Gilbert Rose, Maurice Sendak, Kate Slater, Victoria Ford Smith, Nina Stagakis, Harry Stecopoulos, Bjørn Sundmark, Jan Susina, Sara van den Bossche, Chris Ware, Ed Welter, Karin Westman, Wendy Wick Reaves, and Han Yu.

Sources for Each Chapter

Because all the *Harold* books except for *A Picture for Harold's Room* are unpaginated, I have not listed them in this section. They are, however, in the main References list.

Introduction

This chapter title is an homage to Paul Karasik and Mark Newgarden's *How to Read Nancy: The Elements of Comics in Three Easy Panels* (Fantagraphics, 2017).

Neal Karlen, *This Thing Called Life: Prince's Odyssey, On + Off the Record* (St. Martin's Press, 2020), 30–31; Elizabeth Flock, "Why Richard Powers Schedules His Writing around What Nature Is Doing," *PBS News Hour*, November 18, 2019; Chris Van Allsburg, "*Jumanji*: Caldecott Acceptance Speech."

Tzofit Goldfarb, "Re: Questions about Harold," email to author, June 26, 2023.

Deborah Solomon, "Beyond Finger Paint," *New York Times Book Review*, May 17, 1998.

Nathalie op de Beeck, *Suspended Animation: Children's Picturebooks and the Fairy Tale of Modernity* (University of Minnesota Press, 2010), xii; William Moebius, "Picture Book," in *Keywords for Children's Literature*, 2nd ed., ed. Philip Nel, Lissa Paul, and Nina Christensen (New York University Press, 2021), 142; Barbara Bader, *American Picturebooks from Noah's Ark to the Beast Within* (Macmillan, 1976), 1.

Jenny Odell, *How to Do Nothing: Resisting the Attention Economy* (Melville House, 2019), 154.

"Art Museum Attendance," *American Academy of Arts and Sciences*, <https://www.amacad.org/humanities-indicators/public-life/art-museum-attendance>; Alison Flood, "Britain has closed almost 800 libraries since 2010, figures show," *The Guardian*, December 5, 2019; Brewster Kahle, "The US Library System, Once the Best in the World, Faces Death by a Thousand Cuts," *The Guardian*, October 9, 2023; Shaun Tan, "The Purposeful Daydream: Thoughts on Children's Literature," *Iowa Review* 45, no. 2 (Fall 2015), 115.

Chapter 1

"Harold at the North Pole," press release, HarperCollins, 1998.

Louis W. Bondy, *Miniature Books: Their History from Beginnings to the Present Day* (Sheppard Press, 1981), 78–80; Veryeri Alaca, "Materiality in Picturebooks," in *The Routledge Companion to Picturebooks*, ed. Bettina Kümmerling-Meibauer (Routledge, 2017), 62.

Crockett Johnson, "'THE FIVE-INCH SHELF': Tiny Golden Books as Miniature 'Sets of Classics' for Younger Children," Ruth Krauss Papers, Northeast Children's Literature Collection, Dodd Center, University of Connecticut.

Chapter 2

Catherine de Zegher, "A Century under the Sign of Line: Drawing and Its Extension (1910–2010)," in *On Line: Drawing through the Twentieth Century*, ed. Cornelia H. Butler and Catherine de Zegher (Museum of Modern Art, 2010), 38.

Paul Klee, *Pedagogical Sketchbook*, translated by Sibyl Moholy-Nagy (Praeger Publishers, 1972), 16, 47, 42.

Klee, *Paul Klee Notebooks vol. 1: The Thinking Eye*, translated by Ralph Manheim (Lund Humphries, 1961), 76.

Chapter 3

Crockett Johnson, paste-ups for *Harold and the Purple Crayon*, Ruth Krauss Papers, Northeast Children's Literature Collection, Dodd Center, University of Connecticut; Harolds for *Harold's ABC*, Crockett Johnson Papers, Mathematics Division, NMAH, Smithsonian Institution.

Philip Nel, "'Never overlook the art of the seemingly simple': Crockett Johnson and the Politics of the Purple Crayon," *Children's Literature* 29 (2001), 143.

Chapter 4

Leonard Marcus, "Re: Garamond typeface and Harper," email to author, March 6, 2017; Simon Garfield, *Just My Type: A Book About Fonts* (Penguin, 2012), 92, 4, 92, 51–52.

Chapter 5

Crockett Johnson, *Barnaby, Volume Four: 1948–1949* (Fantagraphics, 2020), 206.

Dave Marion, "Draws Anything," *Journal & Sentinel* (Winston Salem), November 13, 1955; Johnson, letter to Ursula Nordstrom. n.d. but after November 13, 1955, Crockett Johnson Papers, HarperCollins Archives.

Chapter 6

Manfredo di Robilant and Niklas Maak, *Window* (Marsilio, 2014), 8.

Chapter 7

Robin Bernstein, *Racial Innocence: Performing American Childhood from Slavery to Civil Rights* (New York University Press, 2011), 11–13; Helen M. Lothian, letter to Crockett Johnson, March 13, 1958, Crockett Johnson Papers, HarperCollins Archives; Johnson, letter to Helen M. Lothian, April 13, 1958, Crockett Johnson Papers, HarperCollins Archives; Johnson, letter to Ursula Nordstrom, April 13, 1958, Crockett Johnson Papers, HarperCollins Archives.

Johnson, letter to Ursula Nordstrom, April 13, 1958; Joyce Elliott, "JOHNSON, Crockett. Harold's Fairy Tale," *Library Journal*, December 1956; Margaret

Sherwood Libby, "For Boys and Girls," *New York Herald Tribune*, September 23, 1956. Both reviews in Johnson's clippings at HarperCollins Archives; Peter Turchi, *Maps of the Imagination: The Writer as Cartographer* (Trinity University Press, 2004), 47.

Chapter 8

Leonard Marcus, *Dear Genius*, 83, 84; Philip Nel, *Crockett Johnson and Ruth Krauss: How an Unlikely Couple Found Love, Dodged the FBI, and Transformed Children's Literature* (University Press of Mississippi, 2012), 145, 147.

Chapter 9

Jonathan Fineberg, *The Innocent Eye: Children's Art and the Modern Artist* (Princeton University Press, 1997), 2; Nico Laan, "The Making of a Reputation: The Case of Cobra," in *Avant-Garde and Criticism*, ed. K. Beekman and Jan de Vries (Rodopi, 2007), 97–98.

"Kinderwelten/Children's Worlds," *Under the Open Sky: Traveling with Wassily Kandinsky and Gabriele Münter*, exhibition, Lenbachhaus, Munich, Germany, December 14, 2021.

Lee Kingman, Joanna Foster, and Ruth Giles Lontoft, *Illustrators of Children's Books, 1957–1966* (The Horn Book, 1968), 126.

Victoria Ford Smith, *Between Generations: Collaborative Authorship in the Golden Age of Children's Literature* (University Press of Mississippi, 2017), 232.

Chapter 10

As Amy F. Ogata's *Designing the Creative Child: Playthings and Places in Midcentury America* (University of Minnesota Press, 2013) documents, after World War II the inherently creative romantic child gained "new life as an imaginative figure whose natural gifts could be developed through correct parenting, studied, quantified, and assessed in new postwar psychological research, and constituted materially in a wide variety of consumer goods and media" (Ogata 33–34). Quotations all from Ogata, 19, 163, 147, 151, 154.

The analysis in the second paragraph draws on Ogata's *Designing the Creative Child*, 29–30. On Johnson's TV set, see Nel, *Crockett Johnson and Ruth Krauss*, 97.

Chapter 11

Leonard Marcus, ed. *Dear Genius: The Letters of Ursula Nordstrom* (HarperCollins, 1998), 83; Nel, *Crockett Johnson and Ruth Krauss*, 145.

Chapter 12

Maggie Aderin-Pocock, *The Book of the Moon: A Guide to Our Closest Neighbor* (Abrams Image, 2019), 22.

I also learned from NASA's pages on "Lunar Phases and Eclipses" and the "Moon in Motion," as well as Robert Massey and Alexandra Loske's *Moon: Art, Science, Culture* (Ilex, 2018) and Shannon Stirone's "Imagining the Moon," *New York Times*, July 9, 2019.

Johnson, *Barnaby Volume One: 1942–1943* (Fantagraphics Books, 2013), 39.
Nel, *Crockett Johnson and Ruth Krauss*, 67.

Chapter 13

Nel, *Crockett Johnson and Ruth Krauss*, 152.
Kassia St. Clair, *The Secret Lives of Color* (Penguin Books, 2017), 162, 162–163, 166, 169–172, 174.
Ed Welter's magnificent *CrayonCollecting.com* and John W. Kropf's *Color Capital of the World: Growing Up with the Legacy of a Crayon Company* (University of Akron Press, 2022) are the main sources for the third paragraph and, indeed, much of this chapter.
Else Frank, interview with author, Manor Care Health Center, March 20, 2001.
Kropf, *Color Capital of the World*, 23, 25.
Ed Welter, "History of Crayons." *CrayonCollecting.com*.

Chapter 14

Josef Albers, *Interaction of Color*, digital app (Yale University Press & Potion Design, 2013), sections II and XVI.
Molly Bang, *Picture This: How Pictures Work* (Chronicle Books, 2000), 68.

Chapter 15

For any who find *free indirect discourse* a puzzling term, I refer you to M. H. Abrams's succinct definition. It refers

> to the way in many narratives, that the report of what a character says and thinks shift in pronouns, adverbs, tense, and grammatical mode, as we move—or sometimes hover—between the direct narrated reproductions of these events as they occur to the character and the indirect representation of such events by the narrator. Thus, a direct representation, "He thought, 'I will see her home now, and may then stop at my mother's,' might shift, in an indirect representation, to 'He would see her home then, and might afterward stop at his mother's'" (p. 169).

In other words, to shift to free indirect discourse, just change your first-person pronouns to third-person pronouns, and then make any other related shifts (in tone, tense, etc.) that suit your narrative goals.

I borrow the phrase "imagine imagining" from Laura Otis, who in discussing Edwidge Danticat's combination of several senses in *Breath, Eyes, Memory*, says that she "helps readers imagine imagining."

Chapter 16

Immanuel Kant, *The Critique of Judgement*, translated by J. H. Bernard (Macmillan, 1892), 223, 224.
Weston Woods catalogue (Weston Woods, 1969), 12.

Chapter 17

Richard McGuire, "Here," *Comic Art* 8 (Summer 2006), 8–13.

Chapter 18

William C. Dement with Christopher Vaughan, *The Promise of Sleep* (Dell, 1999), 42–45, 58.

Maurice Sendak, *Where the Wild Things Are* (Harper & Row, 1963).

Alan Burdick, *Why Time Flies: A Mostly Scientific Investigation* (Simon & Schuster, Apple eBook edition, 2017), 148, 431.

Lewis Carroll, *Alice's Adventures in Wonderland*, in *The Annotated Alice: The Definitive Edition* (Norton, 2000), 12–13.

Burdick, *Why Time Flies*, 421, 423.

Chapter 19

Marah Gubar, "Risky Business," 454; "A Hole Is to Dig? Harold Should Know," *New Haven Register*, July 12, 1959, 2.

Nel, *Crockett Johnson and Ruth Krauss*, 143–144.

Chapter 20

This chapter is indebted to W. J. T. Mitchell's "Metapictures," in *Picture Theory: Essays on Verbal and Visual Representation* (University of Chicago Press, 1994), 35–82.

Chapter 21

Gene Deitch, letter to Crockett Johnson, June 22, 1973, Northeast Children's Literature Collection, Ruth Krauss Papers; Deitch, "Crockett," email to author, October 28, 2000.

"Gene Deitch: The Picture Book Animated," directed by Gene Deitch (film, 1977).

Chapter 22

Perry Nodelman, "Decoding the Images: How Picture Books Work," in *Understanding Children's Literature*, 2nd ed., ed. Peter Hunt (Routledge, 2005), 132.

Scott McCloud, *Understanding Comics: The Invisible Art* (HarperCollins, 1994), 30.

Chapter 23

Daniel Harris, "Cuteness," *Salmagundi* no. 96 (Fall 1992), 182; Lori Merish, "Cuteness and Commodity Aesthetics: Tom Thumb and Shirley Temple," in *Freakery: Cultural Spectacles of the Extraordinary Body*, edited by Rosemarie Garland Thompson (New York University Press, 1996), 194.

Reviewing *Harold at the North Pole*, the *San Francisco Chronicle* (November 9, 1958) calls Harold an "adventurous moppet." Ellen Lewis Buell, reviewing *Harold's Fairy Tale* for *The New York Times Book Review* (October 21, 1956), calls Harold an "ingenious moppet." The *Chicago Sunday Tribune Magazine of Books* (November 4, 1956) says of *Harold's Fairy Tale* that Harold is "a delightful small scamp." Ellen Lewis Buell, reviewing *Harold's Circus* for *The New York Times Book Review* (April 12, 1959), calls Harold a "saucer-eyed little boy."

Reviewing the same book for *The Chicago Tribune* (April 26, 1959), Polly Goodwin calls him a "saucer-eyed small boy."

Sianne Ngai, *Our Aesthetic Categories: Zany, Cute, Interesting* (Harvard University Press, 2012), 40, 64, 87.

Johnson, *The Blue Ribbon Puppies* (Harper & Row, 1958), 2, 4.

Chapter 24

Chris Ware, "Foreword," *Barnaby Volume One: 1942–1943* (Fantagraphics Books, 2013), 7; Mairead Case, "Draw Us Lines: Reading Harold and the Purple Crayon," *BookSlut*, May 2015; Rachel Skrlac Lo, "Resisting Gentle Bias: A Critical Content Analysis of Family Diversity in Picturebooks," *Journal of Children's Literature* 45, no. 2 (2019), 22–23.

Johnson, paste-ups for *Harold and the Purple Crayon*, Ruth Krauss Papers, Northeast Children's Literature Collection; Mark Newgarden, "Re: Purple Crayons, Nightmare Neighbors, etc.," email to author, September 10, 2014.

Johnson, "Wonderfullums, Inc.," *New Masses*, January 2, 1940, 28; Nel, *Crockett Johnson and Ruth Krauss*, 79, 88, 162.

Brown v. Board of Education of Topeka, Opinion, May 17, 1954, Records of the Supreme Court of the United States, Record Group 267, National Archives.

Rita Dove, "Rita Dove," in *For the Love of Books: 115 Celebrated Writers on the Books They Love Most*, ed. Ronald B. Shwartz (Grosset/Putnam, 1999), 70; Dove, "Maple Valley Branch Library, 1967," in *On the Bus with Rosa Parks* (W. W. Norton & Company, 1999), 32.

Prince, "Purple Rain," *Purple Rain* (Warner Bros., 1984); Neal Karlen, *This Thing Called Life: Prince's Odyssey, On + Off the Record* (St. Martin's Press, 2020), 30–31; Prince and Dan Piepenbring, *The Beautiful Ones* (Spiegel & Grau, 2019), 118; Prince, "Purple Music," *1999*, Super Deluxe Edition (NPG Records/Warner Bros., 2019).

Chapter 25

Linguistic and cultural knowledge courtesy of Björn Sundmark (Swedish), Nina Christensen (Danish), Mervi Pakaste (Finnish), Han Yu (Chinese), Sara van den Bossche (Dutch/Netherlands), and Vanessa Joosen (Dutch/Belgium).

Johnson, *Harald och den Lila Kritan* (Modernista, 2018); Johnson, *Pelle och den roda kirtan* (Natur och Kultur, 1958); Johnson, *Tullemand og det Violette Farvekridt* (Gyldendal, 2000); Johnson, *Paultje en het paarse krijtje* (Lemniscaat, 2000); Johnson, *Valtteri ja Violetti Väriliitu* (Pieni Karhu, 1999).

Walter Benjamin, "The Task of the Translator," in *Illuminations: Essays and Reflections*, translated by Harry Zohn (Schocken Books, 1985), 73, 76; Johnson, *Ich mach mir meine eigne Welt* (Moritz Schauenburg, c. 170); Johnson, *Harold und die Zauberkreide* (Carl Hanser Verlag, 2012).

Rick Farley, "Questions about Harold," email to author, July 17, 2023; Farley, "Re: Questions about Harold, email to Tzofit Goldfarb, July 13, 2023.

Chapter 26

"Memo from Director [J. Edgar Hoover], FBI to SAC, New Haven, June 2, 1950"; "Memo from SAC, New Haven to Director, FBI, December 20, 1954"; "Memo from SAC, New Haven FBI to Director, FBI, February 24, 1955"; "Memo from SAC, New Haven FBI to Director, FBI, April 22, 1955"; and "Memo from Director, FBI to SAC, New Haven, May 16, 1955," all in FBI File for David Johnson Leisk alias Crockett Johnson, 1950–1954.

Communist Party USA Records, Library of Congress; A. B. Magil, telephone interview with author, July 19, 2001.

Nel, *Crockett Johnson and Ruth Krauss*, 103–104.

Julia Mickenberg and Philip Nel, *Tales for Little Rebels: A Collection of Radical Children's Literature* (New York University Press, 2008), 137; Percy Bysshe Shelley, "A Defence of Poetry," in *Shelley's Poetry and Prose*, ed. Donald H. Reiman and Sharon B. Powers (Norton, 1977), 488, 508.

Chapter 27

Ware, "Foreword," *Barnaby Volume One: 1942–1943*, 7; Lisa Belkin, "Children's Books You (Might) Hate," *New York Times Blog*, September 8, 2010; Genevieve, comment on Belkin's "Children's Books You (Might) Hate."

Claire Bartholome, "Harold and the Purple Crayon," *The Prindle Institute*, 2020.

Chapter 28

Nel, *Crockett Johnson and Ruth Krauss*, 191–193, 257; Ron Howard and Clint Howard, *The Boys: A Memoir of Hollywood and Family* (HarperCollins, 2021), 48.

Ann Jorgensen, "NEW HAROLD MS," August 3, 1959, Crockett Johnson Papers, HarperCollins Archives.

Johnson, letter to Ursula Nordstrom, December 11, 1960, Crockett Johnson Papers, HarperCollins Archives.

Susan Carr, jacket copy for *Harold's Republic*, April 19, 1961, Crockett Johnson Papers, HarperCollins Archives.

Chapter 29

Portions of this chapter are adapted from "A Manifesto for Children's Literature; or, Reading Harold as a Teen-Ager," *Iowa Review* 45, no. 2 (Fall 2015), 87–92.

Chapter 30

Nel, *Crockett Johnson and Ruth Krauss*, 149.

Rita Dove, "Rita Dove," *For the Love of Books: 115 Celebrated Writers on the Books They Love Most* (1999), 70; David Freedberg, "Fear of Art: How Censorship Becomes Iconoclasm," *Social Research* 83, no. 1 (Spring 2016), 68.

Afterword

Mark Monmonier, quoted in Turchi, *Maps of the Imagination*, 73.

Linda Hutcheon, *A Theory of Adaptation* (Routledge, 2006), 10.

Christopher Healy, "Parents' Guide to Harold and the Purple Crayon: Wonderful adaptation allows kids to 'be' Harold's crayon," *Common Sense Media; Harold and the Purple Crayon* by Crockett Johnson (app, Trilogy Studios, 2011).

Chris Van Allsburg, "I Could Create My Own World," in *Everything I Need to Know I Learned from a Children's Book*, ed. Anita Silvey (Roaring Brook Press, 2009), 113.

Van Allsburg, *Bad Day at Riverbend* (Houghton Mifflin, 1995).

Dav Pilkey, *The Adventures of Captain Underpants* (Scholastic, 1997), 11, 12, 68, 80–97.

"Top 10 Most Challenged Books Lists," American Library Association; Maurice Sendak, "Let The Kid Do His Own Thing," in *Everything I Need to Know I Learned from a Children's Book*, ed. Anita Silvey (Roaring Brook Press, 2009), 113.

Jon Ehrlich, letter to Ruth Krauss, November 6, 1990, Ruth Krauss Papers, Northeast Children's Literature Collection; Jane Shepherd, prefatory note to Shepherd, Ehrlich, and Pogrebin, *Harold and the Purple Crayon* (Theatreworks USA, 1992); Jon Ehrlich, telephone interview with Philip Nel, October 24, 2009.

Michael Tolkin, *Harold and the Purple Crayon* (unproduced screenplay, c. 1995), 13, 19, 25–26.

Raimund Krumme, "The View from Hollywood," *Animation World Network*, c. 1996.

James Baldwin, *Nobody Knows My Name* (Vintage, 1961), 12.

Wyatte Grantham-Philips and Marc Malkin, "'Harold and the Purple Crayon' Heads to Broadway with Music by AJR (EXCLUSIVE)"; Suerynn Lee, "Harold, I'm Really Going to Need You to Sign the Divorce Papers in Blue or Black Ink," *New Yorker*, August 24, 2020.

D. Gilson, "Harold and the Purple Crayon" (*Poetry*, May 2017).

Nel, "Donald and the Golden Crayon"; P. Shauers, *Donald and the Golden Crayon* (Schiffer Publishing, 2018).

John Darkow, "Donald and the Black Sharpie," *Columbia Missourian*, September 6, 2019; Dana Millbank and Tom Toles, "Donald and the Black Sharpie," *Washington Post*, September 6, 2019; Jake Tapper, "Donald and the Black Sharpie," *CNN*, September 8, 2019; Jimmy Kimmel, "Donald and the Magic Sharpie," *Jimmy Kimmel Live!*, September 6, 2019; Ward Sutton, "Donald and the Purple Sharpie," *The Boston Globe*, September 16, 2019.

"Harold and the Purple Crayon" (episode 1), *Harold and the Purple Crayon* (HBO Family Channel, 2001); Lana Berkowitz, "Youngsters Will Find 'Crayon' Easy to Follow," *Houston Chronicle*, January 4, 2002; "Kid Stuff," *TV Guide*, June 1, 2002, 10.

"The Purple Crayon of Yale"; Amy E. Seham, *Whose Improv Is It Anyway?: Beyond Second City* (University Press of Mississippi, 2001), 49; Matt Fotis, *Long Form Improvisation and American Comedy: The Harold* (Palgrave Macmillan, 2014), 50–51.

Amy Bruckman, "Re: research question: Harold and the Purple Media MOO," email to author, February 21, 2022; Bruckman, "Community Support for Constructionist Learning," *Computer Supported Cooperative Work: The Journal of Collaborative Computing*, no. 7 (1998), 47, 51–52.

Harold and the Purple Crayon Game, designed by Kingsley and Ammon (Briarpatch, Inc., 2001).

Van Allsburg, "I Could Create My Own World," 113; Thacher Hurd, *Art Dog* (HarperCollins, 1996); Hurd, "Re: Crockett Johnson and Ruth Krauss," email to author, June 19, 2005.

Aaron Becker, *Journey* (Candlewick, 2013).

James Preller, "5 QUESTIONS with AARON BECKER, creator of 'JOURNEY,'" *James Preller's Blog*, November 29, 2016.

Edward McLachlan, *Simon in the Land of Chalk Drawings* (Brockhampton Press, 1969); McLachlan, *Simon in the Land of Chalk Drawings: Four Stories That Inspired the TV Series!* (Dover, 2016).

Aaron Reynolds and Peter Brown, *Creepy Crayon!* (Simon & Schuster, 2022); Shoshanah Flax, "Review of *Creepy Crayon!*" *The Horn Book*, October 10, 2022; John Green, *The Anthropocene Reviewed: Essays on a Human-Centered Planet* (Dutton, 2021), 6.

J. M. Barrie, *Peter Pan in Kensington Gardens* and *Peter and Wendy* (Oxford University Press, 1991), 73; Ebony Elizabeth Thomas, *The Dark Fantastic: Race and the Imagination from Harry Potter to the Hunger Games* (New York University Press, 2019), 165, 166.

"The Bob Next Door," *The Simpsons*, Season 21, episode 22, May 16, 2010; "LEGENDS 2014 Window Designers," *La Cienega Design Quarter*; "Compas, Window Designed by Madeline Stuart Based on the Book 'Harold and the Purple Crayon'"; Jerry Scott and Jim Borgman, *Zits*, February 1, 2009.

References

"A Hole Is to Dig? Harold Should Know." *New Haven Register*, July 12, 1959: 2.

Abrams, M. H. *A Glossary of Literary Terms*, 6th ed. Harcourt Brace Jovanovich, 1993.

Aderin-Pocock, Maggie. *The Book of the Moon: A Guide to Our Closest Neighbor.* New York: Abrams Image, 2019.

Agee, Jon. *The Incredible Painting of Felix Clousseau.* Farrar, Straus & Giroux, 1988.

Ahlberg, Allan, and Bruce Ingman. *The Pencil.* Cambridge, Mass.: Candlewick Press, 2008.

Alaca, Veryeri. "Materiality in Picturebooks." In *The Routledge Companion to Picturebooks*, edited by Bettina Kümmerling-Meibauer, 59–68. London: Routledge, 2017.

Albers, Josef. *Interaction of Color.* 1963. Digital app. Yale University Press & Potion Design, 2013.

"Art Museum Attendance." *American Academy of Arts and Sciences.* <https://www.amacad.org/humanities-indicators/public-life/art-museum-attendance>. c. 2019.

Bader, Barbara. *American Picturebooks from Noah's Ark to the Beast Within.* New York: Macmillan, 1976.

Baldwin, James. *Nobody Knows My Name: More Notes of a Native Son.* First published 1961. New York: Vintage, 1993.

Bang, Molly. *Picture This: How Pictures Work.* Chronicle Books, 2000.

Barrie, J. M. *Peter Pan in Kensington Gardens* and *Peter and Wendy.* Edited with an introduction and notes by Peter Hollindale. Oxford University Press, 1991.

Bartholome, Claire. "Harold and the Purple Crayon." *The Prindle Institute*, 2020. <https://www.prindleinstitute.org/books/harold-and-the-purple-crayon/>.

Becker, Aaron. *Journey.* Candlewick Press, 2013.

Becker, Aaron. *Quest.* Candlewick Press, 2014.

Becker, Aaron. *Return.* Candlewick Press, 2016.

Belkin, Lisa. "Children's Books You (Might) Hate." Motherlode. *New York Times Blog*, September 8, 2010. <http://parenting.blogs.nytimes.com/2010/09/08/childrens-books-you-might-hate/>.

Benjamin, Walter. "The Task of the Translator." In *Illuminations: Essays and Reflections*, edited and with an Introduction by Hannah Arendt, translated by Harry Zohn, 69–82. First published 1968. New York: Schocken Books, 1985.

Berkowitz, Lana. "Youngsters Will Find 'Crayon' Easy to Follow." *Houston Chronicle*, January 4, 2002.

Bernstein, Robin. *Racial Innocence: Performing American Childhood from Slavery to Civil Rights.* New York University Press, 2011.

"The Bob Next Door." *The Simpsons.* Season 21, episode 22. Written by John Frink. Directed by Nancy Kruse. Fox. May 16, 2010.

Bondy, Louis W. *Miniature Books: Their History from Beginnings to the Present Day*. London: Sheppard Press, 1981.

Brown v. Board of Education of Topeka. Opinion. May 17, 1954. Records of the Supreme Court of the United States. Record Group 267. National Archives. <https://catalog.archives.gov/id/1656510>.

Brown, Margaret Wise. *Goodnight Moon*. Pictures by Clement Hurd. New York: Harper & Brothers, 1947.

Browne, Anthony. *Bear Hunt*. 1979. London: Picture Puffins, 1994.

Bruckman, Amy. "Community Support for Constructionist Learning." *Computer Supported Cooperative Work: The Journal of Collaborative Computing* Vol. 7 (1998): 47–86.

Bruckman, Amy. "Re: research question: Harold and the Purple Media MOO." Email to author. February 21, 2022.

Burdick, Alan. *Why Time Flies: A Mostly Scientific Investigation*. Apple eBook edition. New York: Simon & Schuster, 2017.

Burningham, John. *Mr. Gumpy's Outing*. Jonathan Cape, 1970.

Carr, Susan. Jacket copy for *Harold's Republic*. April 19, 1961. Crockett Johnson Papers. HarperCollins Archives.

Carroll, Lewis. "Alice's Adventures in Wonderland." In *The Annotated Alice: The Definitive Edition* with Introduction and Notes by Martin Gardner, 1–127. New York: Norton, 2000.

Case, Mairead. "Draw Us Lines: Reading Harold and the Purple Crayon." *BookSlut*. May 2015. <https://web.archive.org/web/20150906061208/https://www.bookslut.com/features/2015_05_021208.php>.

"Chris Van Allsburg: Books I Remember." *HomeArts*, 1995. <https://web.archive.org/web/19961220230607/http://homearts.com/depts/relat/allsbub1.htm>.

Chute, Hillary L. *Outside the Box: Interviews with Contemporary Cartoonists*. Chicago and London: University of Chicago Press, 2014.

Communist Party U.S.A. Records, Library of Congress, Washington, DC.

"Compas, Window Designed by Madeline Stuart Based on the Book 'Harold and the Purple Crayon'." c. May 2014. <https://www.pinterest.com/pin/429812358160178498/>.

Crago, Maureen, and Hugh Crago. *Prelude to Literacy: A Preschool Child's Encounter with Picture and Story*. Southern Illinois University Press, 1983.

Darkow, John. "Donald and the Black Sharpie." *Columbia Missourian*, September 6, 2019. <https://www.columbiamissourian.com/donald-and-the-black-sharpie/image_ff14691e-d012-11e9-ada0-3f22ec436ef9.html>.

de Zegher, Catherine. "A Century Under the Sign of Line: Drawing and Its Extension (1910–2010)." In *On Line: Drawing Through the Twentieth Century*, edited by Cornelia H. Butler and M. Catherine de Zegher, 21–124. New York: Museum of Modern Art, 2010.

Deitch, Gene. Letter to Crockett Johnson. June 22, 1973. Northeast Children's Literature Collection, Ruth Krauss Papers, Series V, Box 22, Folder 724.

Deitch, Gene. "Crockett." Email to author. October 28, 2000.

Deloria, Philip J. *Playing Indian*. New Haven and London: Yale University Press, 1998.

Dement, William C., with Christopher Vaughan. *The Promise of Sleep: A Pioneer in Sleep Medicine Explores the Vital Connection Between Health, Happiness, and a Good Night's Sleep*. Dell, 1999.

di Robilant, Manfredo, and Niklas Maak. *Window.* Book in *Elements of Architecture* series by Rem Koolhaas, AMO, Harvard Graduate School of Design; James Westcott, Editor in Chief; Art Direction and Design by Irma Boom. Italy: Marsilio, 2014.

Dove, Rita. "Maple Valley Branch Library, 1967." In *On the Bus with Rosa Parks*, 32–33. New York: W. W. Norton & Company, 1999.

Dove, Rita. "Rita Dove." In *For the Love of Books: 115 Celebrated Writers on the Books They Love Most*, edited by Ronald B. Shwartz, 70–75. New York: Grosset/Putnam, 1999.

Ehrlich, Jon. Letter to Ruth Krauss. November 6, 1990. Ruth Krauss Papers. Northeast Children's Literature Collection. Dodd Center. University of Connecticut.

Ehrlich, Jon. Telephone interview with Philip Nel. October 24, 2009.

Elliott, Joyce. "JOHNSON, Crockett. Harold's Fairy Tale." *The Library Journal*, December? 1956. Clipping from HarperCollins Archives.

Farley, Rick. "Questions about Harold." Email to author. July 17, 2023.

Farley, Rick. "Re: Questions about Harold." Email to Tzofit Goldfarb. July 13, 2023.

FBI File for David Johnson Leisk alias Crockett Johnson. 1950–1954. File No. 100-HQ-369616. FOIPA No. 0999494-000.

Fineberg, Jonathan. *The Innocent Eye: Children's Art and the Modern Artist.* Princeton, NJ: Princeton University Press, 1997.

Flax, Shoshanah. "Review of *Creepy Crayon!*" *The Horn Book*, October 10, 2022.

Flock, Elizabeth. "Why Richard Powers Schedules His Writing Around What Nature Is Doing." *PBS News Hour*, November 18, 2019. <https://www.pbs.org/newshour/arts/why-richard-powers-compares-his-writing-process-to-a-petri-dish>.

Flood, Alison. "Britain Has Closed Almost 800 Libraries Since 2010, Figures Show." *The Guardian*, December 5, 2019. <https://www.theguardian.com/books/2019/dec/06/britain-has-closed-almost-800-libraries-since-2010-figures-show>.

Fotis, Matt. *Long Form Improvisation and American Comedy: The Harold.* New York: Palgrave Macmillan, 2014.

Frank, Else. Interview with author. Manor Care Health Center, King of Prussia, PA. March 20, 2001.

Freedberg, David. "Fear of Art: How Censorship Becomes Iconoclasm." *Social Research* 83, no. 1 (Spring 2016): 67–99.

Friedman, Lisa, and Mark Walker. "Hurricane Tweet That Angered Trump Wasn't About Trump, Forecasters Say." *New York Times*, November 7, 2019. <https://www.nytimes.com/2019/11/07/climate/trump-alabama-sharpie-hurricane.html>.

Gale, Matthew. *The EY Exhibition: Paul Klee-Making Visible.* Tate Modern. Date of access: August 11, 2014. <https://web.archive.org/web/20140703144500/http://www.tate.org.uk/whats-on/tate-modern/exhibition/ey-exhibition-paul-klee-making-visible>.

Garfield, Simon. *Just My Type: A Book About Fonts.* First published 2010. New York: Penguin, 2012.

Geiger, A. W. "Millennials Are the Most Likely Generation of Americans to Use Public Libraries." *PEW Research Center*, June 21, 2017. <https://www.pewresearch.org/short-reads/2017/06/21/millennials-are-the-most-likely-generation-of-americans-to-use-public-libraries/>.

Gelb, Richard, and Peter Brown. Letter to Ruth Krauss. November 1, 1989. Estate of Ruth Krauss.

"Gene Deitch: The Picture Book Animated." 26-minute film. Directed by Gene Deitch. Weston Woods, 1977.

Genevieve. "Comment on Lisa Belkin's 'Children's Books You (Might) Hate.'" Motherlode. *New York Times Blog*, September 11, 2010. <http://parenting. blogs.nytimes.com/2010/09/08/childrens-books-you-might-hate/?_php= true&_type=blogs&_r=0>.

Gilson, D. "Harold and the Purple Crayon." *Poetry*, May 2017. <https://www. poetryfoundation.org/poetrymagazine/poems/118554/harold-the-purple-crayon>.

Goldfarb, Tzofit. "Re: Questions About Harold." Email to author. June 26, 2023.

Grantham-Philips, Wyatte, and Marc Malkin. "'Harold and the Purple Crayon' Heads to Broadway With Music by AJR (EXCLUSIVE)." *Variety*, Mar. 11, 2022. <https://variety.com/2022/legit/news/harold-and-the-purple-crayon-broadway-ajr-1235202119/>.

Green, John. *The Anthropocene Reviewed: Essays on a Human-Centered Planet*. Dutton, 2021.

Gubar, Marah. "Risky Business: Talking About Children in Children's Literature Criticism." *The Lion and the Unicorn* 38, no. 4 (Winter 2013): 450–457.

Gumbs, Alexis Pauline. *Undrowned: Black Feminist Lessons from Marine Mammals*. AK Press, 2020.

"Harold and the Purple Crayon." Directed by David Piel. Narration by Norman Rose. Music by Jimmy Carroll. Produced by David Piel, Robert Sagalyn, and Stanley Fink. Brandon Films, 1959.

"Harold and the Purple Crayon." 13 episodes. Narration by Sharon Stone. Perf. Connor Matheus, Spencer Breslin, James Sie. HBO Family Channel, 2001–2002.

"Harold and the Purple Crayon." iPad edition. Trilogy Studios, 2011.

"Harold and the Purple Crayon Game". Designed by Peter Kingsley and Rachel Ammon. Briarpatch, Inc., 2001.

"Harold at the North Pole." Press release. HarperCollins, 1998. <https://web. archive.org/web/19990209144213/http://www.harpercollins.com/catalog/ children/0060280735.htm>.

Harris, Daniel. "Cuteness." *Salmagundi* no. 96 (Fall 1992): 177–186.

Healy, Christopher. "Parents' Guide to Harold and the Purple Crayon: Wonderful Adaptation Allows Kids to 'Be' Harold's Crayon." Common Sense Media, c. 2011. <https://www.commonsensemedia.org/app-reviews/harold-and-the-purple-crayon>.

Hopp, Zinken. *The Magic Chalk*. Illus. by Malvin Neset. Translated by Susanne H. Bergendahl. New York: D. McKay Co., 1959.

Hopp, Zinken. *Trollkrittet*. Illus. by Malvin Neset. Bergen, Norway: J.W. Eide, 1948.

Howard, Ron, and Clint Howard. *The Boys: A Memoir of Hollywood and Family*. HarperCollins, 2021.

Hurd, Thacher. *Art Dog*. HarperCollins, 1996.

Hurd, Thacher. "Re: Crockett Johnson and Ruth Krauss." Email to author. June 19, 2005.

Hutcheon, Linda. *A Theory of Adaptation.* New York and London: Routledge, 2006.

Johnson, Crockett. *A Picture for Harold's Room.* New York: Harper, 1960.

Johnson, Crockett. *Barnaby Volume One: 1942–1943.* Edited by Philip Nel and Eric Reynolds. Seattle: Fantagraphics Books, 2013.

Johnson, Crockett. *Barnaby Volume Four: 1948–1949.* Edited by Philip Nel and Eric Reynolds. Seattle: Fantagraphics Books, 2020.

Johnson, Crockett. *The Blue Ribbon Puppies.* Harper & Row, 1958.

Johnson, Crockett. "'THE FIVE-INCH SHELF': Tiny Golden Books as Miniature 'Sets of Classics' for Younger Children." Ruth Krauss Papers. Northeast Children's Literature Collection. Dodd Center. Storrs, CT: University of Connecticut.

Johnson, Crockett. *Harald och den Lila Kritan.* Translated by Eva Håkansson. Stockholm: Modernista, 2018.

Johnson, Crockett. *Harold and the Purple Crayon.* New York: Harper & Brothers, 1955.

Johnson, Crockett. *Harold at the North Pole.* New York: Harper & Brothers, 1958.

Johnson, Crockett. *Harold et le crayon rose.* Translated by Anne-Laure Fournier le Ray. Pocket Jeunesse, 2001.

Johnson, Crockett. *Harold's ABC.* New York: Harper & Brothers, 1963.

Johnson, Crockett. *Harold's Circus.* New York: Harper & Brothers, 1959.

Johnson, Crockett. *Harold's Fairy Tale.* New York: Harper & Brothers, 1956.

Johnson, Crockett. *Harold's Trip to the Sky.* New York: Harper & Brothers, 1957.

Johnson, Crockett. *Harold und die Zauberkreide.* Translated by Anu Stohner. Munich: Carl Hanser Verlag, 2012.

Johnson, Crockett. "Harolds for Harold's ABC." Crockett Johnson Papers. Mathematics Division, NMAH. Washington, DC: Smithsonian Institution.

Johnson, Crockett. *Ich mach mir meine eigne Welt.* Schwarzwald, Germany: Moritz Schauenburg KG, c. 1970.

Johnson, Crockett. Letter to Helen M. Lothian. April 13, 1958. Crockett Johnson Papers. HarperCollins Archives.

Johnson, Crockett. Letter to Ursula Nordstrom. n.d., but after November 13, 1955. Crockett Johnson Papers. HarperCollins Archives.

Johnson, Crockett. Letter to Ursula Nordstrom. April 13, 1958. Crockett Johnson Papers. HarperCollins Archives.

Johnson, Crockett. Letter to Ursula Nordstrom. December 11, 1960. Crockett Johnson Papers. HarperCollins Archives.

Johnson, Crockett. Paste-ups for Harold and the Purple Crayon. 1954. Ruth Krauss Papers. Northeast Children's Literature Collection. Dodd Center. Storrs. CT: University of Connecticut.

Johnson, Crockett. *Paultje en het paarse krijtje.* Translated by Annie M.G. Schmidt. Rotterdam: Lemniscaat, 2000.

Johnson, Crockett. *Pelle och den roda kirtan.* Translated by Eva Håkanson. Natur och Kultur, 1958.

Johnson, Crockett. *Tullemand og det Violette Farvekridt.* Translated into Danish by Bibi and Thomas Winding. Copenhagen: Gyldendal, 2000.

Johnson, Crockett. *Valtteri ja Violetti Väriliitu.* Translated by Riitta Oittinen. Kärköla. Finland: Pieni Karhu, 1999.

Johnson, Crockett. "Wonderfullums, Inc." *New Masses*, January 2, 1940: 28.

Johnson, Kim "Howard." *The Funniest One in the Room: The Lives and Legends of Del Close.* Chicago Review Press, 2008.

Jorgensen, Ann. "NEW HAROLD MS." August 3, 1959. Readers report on *A Picture for Harold's Room.* Crockett Johnson Papers. HarperCollins Archives.

Kahle, Brewster. "The US Library System, Once the Best in the World, Faces Death by a Thousand Cuts." *The Guardian*, October 9, 2023. <https://www.theguardian.com/commentisfree/2023/oct/09/us-library-system-attack-digital-licensing>.

Kant, Immanuel. *The Critique of Judgement.* Translated by J. H. Bernard. Macmillan, 1892.

Karlen, Neal. *This Thing Called Life: Prince's Odyssey, On + Off the Record.* St. Martin's Press, 2020.

"Kid stuff." TV Guide, June 1, 2002: 10.

Kimmel, Jimmy. "Donald and the Magic Sharpie." *Jimmy Kimmel Live!*, September 6, 2019. <https://www.youtube.com/watch?v=rJOUdC9lqfM>.

"Kinderwelten/Children's Worlds." *Under the Open Sky: Traveling with Wassily Kandinsky and Gabriele Münter.* Exhibition. Lenbachhaus. Munich, Germany. December 14, 2021.

Kingman, Lee, Joanna Foster, and Ruth Giles Lontoft. *Illustrators of Children's Books, 1957–1966.* Boston: The Horn Book, 1968.

Klee, Paul. *Paul Klee Notebooks vol. 1: The Thinking Eye.* Edited by Jürg Spiller. Translated by Ralph Manheim. London: Lund Humphries, 1961.

Klee, Paul. *Pedagogical Sketchbook.* Introduction and Translation by Sibyl Moholy-Nagy. New York and Washington: Praeger Publishers, 1972.

Krauss, Ruth. *The Carrot Seed.* Pictures by Crockett Johnson. New York: Harper & Brothers, 1945.

Kropf, John W. *Color Capital of the World: Growing Up with the Legacy of a Crayon Company.* Akron, Ohio: University of Akron Press, 2022.

Krumme, Raimund. "The View from Hollywood." *Animation World Network*, c. 1996. Date of access: Apr. 20, 2000.<http://www.awn.com/mag/issue1.7/articles/krumme1.7.html>.

Laan, Nico. "The Making of a Reputation: The Case of Cobra." In *Avant-Garde and Criticism*, edited by K. Beekman and Jan de Vries, 92–118. Rodopi, 2007.

Lee, Suerynn. "Harold, I'm Really Going to Need you to Sign the Divorce Papers in Blue or Black Ink." Cartoon. *New Yorker*, August 24, 2020.

"LEGENDS 2014 Window Designers." *La Cienega Design Quarter*, 2014. <https://lcdqla.com/legends-2014-window-designers/>.

Libby, Margaret Sherwood. "For Boys and Girls." *New York Herald Tribune*, September 23, 1956.

Lothian, Helen M. Letter to Crockett Johnson. March 13, 1958. Crockett Johnson Papers. HarperCollins Archives.

"Lunar Phases and Eclipses." *NASA.* Date of access: April 26, 2024. <https://science.nasa.gov/moon/lunar-phases-and-eclipses/>.

Magil, A. B. Telephone interview with Philip Nel. July 19, 2001.

Marcus, Leonard, ed. *Dear Genius: The Letters of Ursula Nordstrom.* New York: HarperCollins, 1998.

Marcus, Leonard. "Re: Garamond typeface and Harper." Email to author. March 6, 2017.

Marion, Dave. "Draws Anything." *Journal & Sentinel* (Winston Salem), November 13, 1955.

Massey, Robert, and Alexandra Loske. *Moon: Art, Science, Culture.* London: Ilex/ Octopus Publishing, 2018.

Mautner, Chris. "Talking Barnaby: An interview with co-editors Eric Reynolds and Phil Nel." *Comic Book Resources*, June 28, 2014. <https://www.cbr.com/ talking-barnaby-an-interview-with-co-editors-eric-reynolds-and-phil-nel/>.

McCloud, Scott. *Understanding Comics: The Invisible Art.* New York: HarperCollins, 1993.

McGuire, Richard. "Here." 1989. Repr. *Comic Art* no. 8 (Summer 2006): 8–13.

McGuire, Richard. *Here.* New York: Pantheon Books, 2014.

McLachlan, Edward. *Simon and the Moon Rocket.* Leicester, Great Britain: Brockhampton Press, 1972.

McLachlan, Edward. *Simon in the Land of Chalk Drawings.* Leicester, Great Britain: Brockhampton Press, 1969.

McLachlan, Edward. *Simon in the Land of Chalk Drawings: Four Stories That Inspired the TV Series!* Dover, 2016.

Merish, Lori. "Cuteness and Commodity Aesthetics: Tom Thumb and Shirley Temple." In *Freakery: Cultural Spectacles of the Extraordinary Body*, edited by Rosemarie Garland Thompson, 185–206. New York University Press, 1996.

Mickenberg, Julia, and Philip Nel, eds. *Tales for Little Rebels: A Collection of Radical Children's Literature.* New York University Press, 2008.

Millbank, Dana, and Tom Toles. "Donald and the Black Sharpie." *Washington Post*, September 6, 2019. <https://www.washingtonpost.com/opinions/donald-and-the-black-sharpie/2019/09/06/44202240-d0b9-11e9-b29b-a528dc82154a_story.html>.

Mitchell, W. J. T. *Picture Theory: Essays on Verbal and Visual Representation.* University of Chicago Press, 1994.

Moebius, William. "Picture Book." In *Keywords for Children's Literature*, 2nd ed., edited by Philip Nel, Lissa Paul, and Nina Christensen, 142–5. New York University Press, 2021.

"Moon in Motion." *NASA.* Date of access: April 26, 2024. <https://moon.nasa. gov/moon-in-motion/phases-eclipses-supermoons/moon-phases/>.

Nel, Philip. *Crockett Johnson and Ruth Krauss: How an Unlikely Couple Found Love, Dodged the FBI, and Transformed Children's Literature.* Jackson: University Press of Mississippi, 2012.

Nel, Philip. "Donald and the Golden Crayon." *Nine Kinds of Pie: Philip Nel's Blog*, October 20, 2018. <https://philnel.com/2018/10/20/donald-and-the-golden-crayon/>.

Nel, Philip. "The Indian in the Comic; or, How to Read Crockett Johnson's *Barnaby* Uncomfortably." Unpublished paper. May 2022.

Nel, Philip. "A Manifesto for Children's Literature; or, Reading Harold as a Teen-Ager." *Iowa Review* 45, no. 2 (Fall 2015): 87–92.

Nel, Philip. "'Never Overlook the Art of the Seemingly Simple': Crockett Johnson and the Politics of the Purple Crayon." *Children's Literature* 29 (2001): 142–74.

Newgarden, Mark. "Re: Purple Crayons, Nightmare Neighbors, etc." Email to author. September 10, 2014.

Ngai, Sianne. *Our Aesthetic Categories: Zany, Cute, Interesting.* Harvard University Press, 2012.

Nodelman, Perry. "Decoding the Images: How Picture Books Work." In *Understanding Children's Literature*, 2nd ed., edited by Peter Hunt, 128–39. Routledge, 2005.

Odell, Jenny. *How to Do Nothing: Resisting the Attention Economy.* Brooklyn: Melville House, 2019.

Ogata, Amy F. *Designing the Creative Child: Playthings and Places in Midcentury America.* Minneapolis and London: University of Minnesota Press, 2013.

Op de Beeck, Nathalie. *Suspended Animation: Children's Picturebooks and the Fairy Tale of Modernity.* University of Minnesota Press, 2010.

Otis, Laura. "Multimodal Imagery: Reading with the Mind's Full Body." Conference paper. *Modern Language Association Convention.* January 4, 2024.

Phillips, Patrick. "Boy Wonder Gets the Purple Crayon." *New York Times*, May 7, 1995: Sec. 1, p. 59.

Pilkey, Dav. *The Adventures of Captain Underpants.* Scholastic, 1997.

Powers, Ann. Reader's report for *Harold and the Purple Crayon.* 1954. Crockett Johnson Papers. HarperCollins Archives.

Preller, James. "5 QUESTIONS with AARON BECKER, creator of 'JOURNEY.'" *James Preller's Blog*, November 29, 2016. <http://www.jamespreller.com/tag/harold-and-the-purple-crayon/>.

Prince. 1999. Super Deluxe Edition. NPG Records/Warner Bros., 2019.

Prince. *Prince: The Last Interview and Other Conversations.* Introduction by Hanif Abdurraqib. Penguin Random House, 2019.

Prince. *Purple Rain.* Warner Bros., 1984.

Prince. *The Beautiful Ones.* Edited with an introduction by Dan Piepenbring. Spiegel & Grau, 2019.

"The Purple Crayon of Yale." *Shakespeare at Yale.* Date of access: April 26, 2024. <https://shakespeare.yale.edu/partners/purple-crayon-yale>.

Rey, H.A. *Curious George.* Boston: Houghton Mifflin Co., 1941.

Reynolds, Aaron, and Peter Brown. *Creepy Crayon!* Simon & Schuster, 2022.

Scott, Jerry, and Jim Borgman. *Zits*, February 1, 2009.

Seham, Amy E. *Whose Improv Is It Anyway?: Beyond Second City.* Jackson: University Press of Mississippi, 2001.

Sendak, Maurice. "Let the kid do his own thing." In *Everything I Need to Know I Learned from a Children's Book: Life Lessons from Notable People from All Walks of Life*, edited by Anita Silvey, 113. New York: Roaring Brook Press, 2009.

Sendak, Maurice. *Where the Wild Things Are.* Harper & Row, 1963.

Shauers, P. *Donald and the Golden Crayon.* Algen, PA: Schiffer Publishing, 2018.

Shelley, Percy Bysshe. "A Defence of Poetry." In *Shelley's Poetry and Prose*, edited by Donald H. Reiman and Sharon B. Powers, 480–508. First published 1821. New York: Norton, 1977.

Shepherd, Jane, Jon Ehrlich, and Robin Pogrebin. *Harold and the Purple Crayon*. Music by Jon Ehrlich, Lyrics by Robin Pogrebin and Jon Ehrlich. Adapted by Jane Shepherd. Final draft of script, dated January 1992. Theatreworks USA, 1992.

Skrlac Lo, Rachel. "Resisting Gentle Bias: A Critical Content Analysis of Family Diversity in Picturebooks." *Journal of Children's Literature* 45, no. 2 (2019): 16–30.

Smith, Victoria Ford. *Between Generations: Collaborative Authorship in the Golden Age of Children's Literature*. Jackson: University Press of Mississippi, 2017.

Solomon, Deborah. "Beyond Finger Paint." *New York Times Book Review*, May 17, 1998: 24–5.

St. Clair, Kassia. *The Secret Lives of Color*. New York: Penguin Books, 2017.

Sterne, Laurence. *The Life and Opinions of Tristram Shandy, Gentleman*. 1759–1767. Edited and with an introduction by Ian Watt. Boston: Houghton Mifflin Company, 1965.

Stirone, Shannon. "Imagining the Moon." *New York Times*, July 9, 2019. <https://www.nytimes.com/2019/07/09/science/moon-art-culture.html>.

Sutton, Ward. "Donald and the Purple Sharpie." *The Boston Globe*, September 16, 2019. <https://www.bostonglobe.com/opinion/2019/09/15/donald-trump-and-purple-sharpie/M0KFbE6WDP8kzZMZieA2aO/story.html>.

Tan, Shaun. "The Purposeful Daydream: Thoughts on Children's Literature." *The Iowa Review* 45, no. 2 (Fall 2015): 100–15.

Tapper, Jake. "Donald and the Black Sharpie." *CNN*, September 8, 2019. <https://www.cnn.com/videos/politics/2019/09/08/sotu-cartoonion-full.cnn>.

"Theatreworks USA presents Harold and the Purple Crayon: a New Musical based on the book by Crockett Johnson." Postcard. Ruth Krauss Papers. Northeast Children's Literature Collection. Dodd Center. Storrs, CT: University of Connecticut.

Thomas, Ebony Elizabeth. *The Dark Fantastic: Race and the Imagination from Harry Potter to the Hunger Games*. New York University Press, 2019.

Tolkin, Michael. "Harold and the Purple Crayon." Unproduced screenplay. c. 1995.

"Top 10 Most Challenged Books Lists." American Library Association. 2023. <https://www.ala.org/advocacy/bbooks/frequentlychallengedbooks/top10/archive>.

Turchi, Peter. *Maps of the Imagination: The Writer as Cartographer*. San Antonio, TX: Trinity University Press, 2004.

Van Allsburg, Chris. *Bad Day at Riverbend*. Boston: Houghton Mifflin, 1995.

Van Allsburg, Chris. "I could create my own world." In *Everything I Need to Know I Learned from a Children's Book: Life Lessons from Notable People from All Walks of Life*, edited by Anita Silvey, 113. New York: Roaring Brook Press, 2009.

Van Allsburg, Chris. "*Jumanji*: Caldecott Acceptance Speech." Given at the meeting of the American Library Association, Philadelphia, July 22, 1982. <https://chris-van-allsburg.harpercollins.com/speeches-and-interviews>.

Ware, Chris. "Foreword." In *Barnaby Volume One: 1942–1943*, edited by Philip Nel and Eric Reynolds, 7–9. Seattle: Fantagraphics Books, 2013.

Welter, Ed. "The Definitive History of the Colors of Crayola." *CrayonCollecting.com*.

Welter, Ed. "History of Crayons." *CrayonCollecting.com*.

Weston Woods catalogue. Weston, CT: Weston Woods, 1969.

Index

For the benefit of digital users, indexed terms that span two pages (e.g., 52–53) may, on occasion, appear on only one of those pages.